PRAIRIE SMALL-TOWN SURVIVAL

The Challenge of Agro-Manitoba

John S. Brierley
Daniel Todd

Canadian Studies
Volume 7

The Edwin Mellen Press
Lewiston/Queenston/Lampeter

Library of Congress Cataloging-in-Publication Data

Brierley, John S.
Prairie small-town survival : the challenge of Agro-Manitoba / John S. Brierley and Daniel Todd.
p. cm. -- (Canadian studies ; v. 7)
Includes bibliographical references.
ISBN 0-88946-211-9
1. Manitoba--Rural conditions. 2. Cities and towns--Manitoba. 3. Agriculture--Social aspects--Manitoba. I. Todd, Daniel. II. Title. III. Series: Canadian studies (Lewiston, N.Y.) ; v. 7.
HN110.M35B74 1990
307.72'097127--dc20 89-13551
CIP

This is volume 7 in the continuing series
Canadian Studies
Volume 7 ISBN 0-88946-211-9
CS Series ISBN 0-88946-197-X

A CIP catalog record for this book
is available from the British Library.

The Edwin Mellen Press
Box 450
Lewiston, New York
USA 14092

The Edwin Mellen Press
Box 67
Queenston, Ontario
CANADA L0S 1L0

Edwin Mellen Press, Ltd
Lampeter, Dyfed, Wales
UNITED KINGDOM SA48 7DY

Printed in the United States of America

PRAIRIE SMALL-TOWN SURVIVAL

The Challenge of Agro-Manitoba

TABLE OF CONTENTS

LIST OF TABLES

LIST OF FIGURES

FOREWORD

Most small towns in the Canadian Prairies owe their genesis to the development of commercial agriculture. Beginning in the 1870s and continuing until 1930, a network of farm-service centres emerged throughout the region catering to the needs of grain and livestock producers. After 1930 the combined effects of, first, low grain prices and poor yields and, then, the advent of extensive combustion-powered mechanization, transformed prairie agriculture by reducing the number of farms while simultaneously increasing their size. As this trend continued unabated, dire consequences were foreseen for many of the smaller rural communities whose symbiotic relationship with a sizeable local farm population had been undermined. Consequently, in the 1960s and 1970s federal and provincial governments undertook initiatives to address the problem. In this study particular attention is given to 58 small towns in Southern Manitoba; a region whose rural economy has remained firmly rooted in agriculture, unlike Saskatchewan and Alberta whose rural economies have benefited from the development of mineral resources. Analysis focuses on the 1971-81 intercensal decade - a period noted throughout North America for its population reversal whereby non-metropolitan centres (small towns) grew at a faster rate than metropolitan areas. Investigation of the economic underpinnings of Agro-Manitoban communities indicates that a fundamental change occurred in the 1970s with manufacturing activity being a stimulus to centres exhibiting viability. However, examination of the social dimension of small towns reveals a disproportionately high number of old people in their populations who are specifically attracted to communities providing a comprehensive set of social services and amenities. Although to date the region's small towns have exhibited a remarkable tenacity to survive and accommodate changes in the economic climate, our conclusions are less sanguine for their futures. On the one hand, there can never be enough manufacturing activities to support all small centres and, on the other, the elderly populations in these towns portend their inevitable decline. These conclusions are deemed germane for other regions whose economies depend on agriculture.

ACKNOWLEDGEMENTS

The authors are grateful to a number of people who willingly assisted them in seeing this work through to fruition. Initial encouragement for this study came from Professor R.J.C. Munton, University College, London, who provided valued comment and criticism to an early draft of the manuscript. We also are indebted to members of the Department of Geography staff: namely, the secretaries Mrs. E. Gaetz, Mrs. H. Chambers, Mrs B. Hendricks and Mrs. J. Michalski, who typed various drafts and the final copy of the text; and the technicians, Mrs. M. Halmarson and Mr. E.Pachanuk, who drew the maps and diagrams.

Finally we are indebted to the University of Manitoba for providing SSHRC funds to assemble and process the data.

Chapter 1

An Historical Perspective of Prairie Settlement

Introduction

A vibrant era of settlement in the Canadian Prairies commenced with the opening up of Canada's grassland interior to commercial wheat farming in the 1870s and continued until 1913. This period was one of unprecedented population increase that derived from the influx of aspiring farmers and the establishment of a network of attendant service centres. It was during these years of spectacular growth that the foundations of the region's settlement pattern were laid down. In contrast, the subsequent history of rural communities was characterized by consolidation and gradual expansion from 1918 until 1930. Since 1930 prairie agriculture has been subject to almost continuous modification in accordance with the vagaries imposed by climate and the market place on the one hand, and the benefits accruing from mechanization and economies of scale on the other. Naturally, the form and function of rural service centres were affected by these changes. Some communities were to thrive and become higher-order centres, others struggled to survive and the least fortunate were to wither. However, census data for the 1970s revealed evidence of small-town revival in North America as growth in metropolitan areas underwent readjustment - a phenomenon known as counter-urbanization. Central to this study is the analysis of the underlying characteristics associated with the varying fortunes on non-metropolitan centres found in Agro-Manitoba for the 1971-81 intercensal period in light of that phenomenon. This sub-region of the Prairies has remained fundamentally unaltered since the 1870s, unlike those for Alberta and Saskatchewan which have the added benefit of development from mineral resources. In order to understand the current state of affairs with respect to rural settlements in areas specializing in agriculture, a review of the social and economic history of the Prairies is provided.

The Period to 1930

In 1870 settlement of the Prairies was largely confined to natural waterways, most notably at strategic points on accessible rivers where the Hudson's Bay Company had located its trading posts. Adjacent to these posts were small farm settlements where little more than subsistence agriculture was practised. Some of these scattered communities, in particular those on the Red, Souris, Qu'Appelle and Saskatchewan Rivers, were the nuclei about which the region's metropolitan centres were to subsequently evolve (Dawson and Younge, 1940). In all, some 70,000 people resided in the region by 1870, but few could be regarded as urban dwellers since the largest centre, with 800 inhabitants, was St. Boniface, a Roman Catholic missionary and educational centre on the Red River across from Winnipeg (Artibise, 1979).

It was the advent of the railroad onto the prairie landscape that opened up the region to mass immigration and the possibilities of commercial agriculture whereby wheat, the region's staple crop, could be competitive in the European market. In 1878 Winnipeg gained railway linkage with St. Paul, Minnesota, and hence with Chicago, and five years later obtained direct connection with eastern Canada via the Canadian Pacific Railway (CPR). Subsequently, branch lines began to proliferate, initially in Manitoba's eastern grasslands and then westwards. By 1931 a comprehensive network served the prairies, together with an additional outlet for grain shipment in the port of Churchill on Hudson Bay (Mackintosh, 1934).

Although the railway was of paramount importance in determining settlement patterns, other factors were significant, not least of which was the Land Act of 1872 which enabled persons with little capital to acquire farmland by homesteading.

> Any man who was head of a family or who reached the age of twenty-one years could apply for a quarter section of land (160 ac or 65 ha) and at the end of three years he could obtain, provided that he had prepared a stipulated portion of this for cultivation and made a modest beginning with respect to

> buildings. A nominal fee of $10 was charged by the local land office (Dawson and Younge, 1940).

Migrants from Eastern Canada, the United States and Europe entered the region in hope of improving their economic lot. Amongst the first groups to settle were German-speaking Mennonites from Russia, whose farming experience in the Steppes enabled them to adapt readily to the open prairie, as distinct from that in the more amenable valley bottoms. They became the pathfinders of commercial agriculture in the prairies. The Dominion Government allocated two blocks of land south of Winnipeg for Mennonites and by 1880 these were occupied by nearly 7000 colonists. Such block settlement enabled this group to maintain its cultural identity which was readily preserved in its towns and villages.

Success of Mennonite block settlement provided the Government with a model by which to settle other ethnic groups. Thus, other special areas were assigned to distinct national and/or ethnic groups to create "a recognizable mosaic of 'ethnic islands' " (Sawatzky, 1970). Although some of these islands eventually lost their cultural stamp through assimilation, others were more closely bound by language and religion.[1] In these "islands" urban centres developed, some to become the foci of commercial and cultural intercourse which, in turn, reinforced their survival and growth.

To this point the relationship between prairie settlement and railroad development has been implied but not detailed. In fact, not only did rural centres spring up along railway lines, but they were established in anticipation of predicted routes. The railway served as an umbilical cord joining the prairies with Canada's Heartland in Southern Ontario. As well as accommodating the flow of migrants and manufactured goods into the region, the railway enabled wheat to enter the international commodity market. Expansion of the rail network created new agricultural hinterlands with their attendant small towns and villages generally positioned at intervals of 14 km along the track where grain elevators were located.[2]

---

[1]Mennonites are a pacifist offshoot of the Anabaptist movement that had its origins in Holland during the sixteenth century. They are noted for their dedication to agriculture (see Sawatzky 1970 for an account of their settlement).

[2]Mackintosh (1934) remarked that, "It is difficult to arrive at any conclusion as to the distance beyond which hauling of grain is unprofitable...however, areas lying more than ten miles [16 km] from the railway have low population density and are not characteristically grain-shipping district."

Larger centres emerged at divisional points on these lines, at intervals of 175 to 210 km, where water for steam locomotives and crews were changed (Sarbit and Greer-Wootten, 1980).

In 1901 approximately 5800 km of rail laced the prairies (Artibise, 1979) and the region's grand population was about 420,000 inhabitants. Despite such development, the pre-1900 era was one of slow progress in comparison to that which occurred between 1900 and 1913. Buoyed by an expanding world market for wheat, rising prices, reduced freight rates, and improved knowledge of how to cope with the agricultural problems inherent in semi-arid areas, prairie development entered a boom phase. Indicative of this expansion was: i) the laying of an additional 11,250 km of railway track, mostly branch lines of the CPR and the two new trans-continental railways, the Canadian National and Grand Trunk Pacific, and ii) the trebling of population to about 1.32 million by 1913. The primate centre, Winnipeg, was a city of 150,000 residents. Table 1.1 reveals the intercensal period 1901 to 1911 to be that of greatest agricultural expansion, with corresponding growth in the number of service centres (Table 1.2). Depending upon their 'central place' status, these centres offered a range of services. Those of low-order were characterized by the "unfailing accompaniments" of the railway, namely, "the loading platform, the two to five grain elevators, the post office, general store, machinery shed, and branch bank" (Mackintosh, 1934), all services vital to the grain-producing infrastructure. Schools and churches were additional features of these communities. With population growth, a sequential expansion of services occurred that invariably included another general store, which, in turn, was augmented by a lumber yard, hardware store, a harness and wagon business and an implement dealer. When centres reached a population of about 1000 inhabitants, they assumed an independence of their own, acquiring less essential services, such as hotels, taverns, cafes, barber shops, recreation centres, and real-estate offices (Voisey, 1975). It was in the highest-order centres, the region's cities, that specialized professional, commercial and industrial services were located. These centres were the hubs of the transportation network, in addition to being sites forthe "region's political and legal institutions (legislatures, court houses, government offices) and educational institutions (universities, trade schools, teacher's colleges)" (Artibise, 1979).

Table 1.1 Prairie Region: Number of Farmers and Area of Farmland Occupied

Census Year	1891	1901	1911	1921	1931	1941	1951	1961	1971	1981
					Number of Farmers (1000s)					
Manitoba	22.8	32.3	43.7	53.3	54.2	58.0	52.4	43.3	35.0	29.4
Saskatchewan	6.7	13.4	95.0	119.5	136.5	138.7	112.0	93.9	77.0	67.3
Alberta	2.6	9.5	60.6	83.0	97.4	99.7	84.3	73.2	62.7	58.1
Total	32.1	55.2	199.3	255.8	288.1	296.4	248.7	210.4	174.7	154.8
% decennial change		72.0	261.1	28.3	12.6	2.9	-16.1	-15.4	-17.0	-11.4
					Area of Farmland (1000 ha)					
Manitoba	-	3379	4931	5915	6123	6833	7175	7353	7693	7616
Saskatchewan	-	1551	11,372	17,816	22,531	24,251	24,955	26,069	26,328	25,948
Alberta	-	1107	7025	11,855	15,774	17,517	17,993	19,114	20,035	20,206
Total	-	6037	23,328	35,586	44,428	48,601	50,135	52,536	54,056	53,770
% decennial change			286.4	52.5	24.8	9.4	3.1	4.8	2.9	-0.5

Sources: 1921 Census of Canada
1936 Census of Prairie Provinces
1961 Census of Canada
1981 Agricultural Censuses of Manitoba, Saskatchewan and Alberta

Table 1.2 Prairie Region: Population Growth 1901-1981

Census Year	1901	1911	1921	1931	1941	1951	1961	1971	1981
				Population in 1000s					
Manitoba	255.2	461.2	610.1	700.1	729.7	776.5	921.7	988.2	1,026.2
Saskatchewan	91.3	492.4	757.5	921.8	896.0	831.0	925.7	926.2	968.3
Alberta	73.0	374.3	588.5	731.6	796.2	939.5	1,332.0	1,627.9	2,237.7
Total	419.5	1,328.1	1,956.1	2,353.5	2,421.9	2,547.0	3,179.4	3,542.3	4,232.2
% decennial increase		216.6	47.3	20.3	2.9	5.2	24.8	11.4	19.5

Source: 1926 Census of the Prairie Provinces, Ottawa
1961-71-81 Population Census of Canada

Table 1.3 Prairie Region: Number of Trade Centres by Size Categories, 1901-1981

Census Year	1901	1911	1921	1931	1941	1951	1961	1971	1981
Size Categories of Trade Centres									
MANITOBA									
200-500	4(17)*	9(12)	11(24)	12(22)	13(23)	16(23)	11(16)	13(16)	13(17)
501-1000	8(35)	18(43)	21(46)	23(42)	25(45)	26(37)	29(43)	37(47)	30(39)
1001-3000	8(35)	11(26)	7(15)	12(22)	11(20)	21(30)	19(28)	15(19)	20(26)
3001-5000	1(4)	-	3(6)	3(5)	2(5)	1(1)	3(4)	6(8)	3(4)
over 5000	2(9)	4(10)	4(9)	5(9)	5(9)	6(9)	6(9)	8(10)	10(13)
Total	**23**	**42**	**46**	**55**	**56**	**70**	**68**	**79**	**76**
SASKATCHEWAN									
201-500	-	77(71)	133(72)	171(71)	169(72)	187(68)	192(63)	162(56)	127(47)
501-1000	3	17(16)	27(15)	39(16)	34(15)	51(19)	63(21)	68(24)	71(27)
1001-3000	3	10(9)	17(9)	23(10)	20(9)	24(9)	35(12)	41(14)	47(18)
3001-5000	-	-	3(2)	1(1)	4(2)	3(1)	4(1)	7(2)	9(3)
over 5000	-	4(4)	5(3)	8(3)	7(3)	8(3)	9(3)	10(4)	13(5)
Total	-	**108**	**185**	**242**	**234**	**273**	**303**	**288**	**268**
ALBERTA									
201-500	9(50)	26(39)	64(55)	68(53)	62(50)	75(46)	84(41)	83(40)	75(34)
501-1000	3(17)	22(33)	27(23)	30(23)	34(27)	39(24)	48(23)	39(19)	35(16)
1001-3000	5(28)	15(22)	22(19)	27(21)	25(20)	43(26)	52(25)	54(26)	59(27)
3001-5000	1(5)	-	-	-	-	2(1)	9(4)	19(9)	23(10)
over 5000	-	4(6)	4(3)	4(3)	4(3)	5(3)	13(6)	13(6)	30(14)
Total	**18**	**67**	**117**	**129**	**125**	**164**	**206**	**208**	**222**
PRAIRIE PROVINCES									
201-500	-	112(15)	208(60)	251(59)	244(59)	278(58)	287(50)	258(45)	215(38)
501-1000	14	59(26)	75(22)	92(22)	93(22)	116(23)	140(24)	144(25)	139(25)
1001-3000	16	36(17)	46(13)	62(14)	56(14)	88(17)	106(18)	110(19)	129(23)
3001-5000	2	-	6(2)	4(1)	6(1)	6(1)	16(3)	32(6)	31(5)
over 5000	2	12(6)	13(4)	17(4)	16(4)	19(4)	28(5)	31(5)	53(9)
Total	-	**216**	**348**	**426**	**415**	**507**	**577**	**575**	**567**

* Number in brackets denotes percentage of total. Source: 1936 Census of the Prairie Provinces 1961-71-81 Population Censuses of Canada

The first 13 years of this century represent the formative periods of small-town development on the prairies. It was the time when the cadre of their service functions and the linkages vital to their survival were established. However, this era of rapid growth and prosperity was interrupted by recession in 1913, the impact of World War I and slow economic recovery thereafter. In the early 1920s the region was afflicted by further recession, inflation, not to speak of drought in the southern prairies that lasted from 1919 to 1924. These influences restricted, but did not curtail, development of farm and urban centres (Tables 1.1 and 1.3).

A brief period of expansion and prosperity affected the region after 1924. During this time immigrants entered the northern frontier of agriculture and the final thrust of railway-line construction was undertaken. As world wheat prices were high, the more progressive farmers could partake in the mechanical revolution. The transition from horse-drawn equipment to self-propelled tractors, combine harvesters and trucks made farmers increasingly dependent on urban services and skills. Renewed vigour and importance in the network of rural centres was the outcome, and it was complemented by the rising importance of roads as a consequence of the diffusion of the private automobile.

By 1929 the mini-boom was over. The onset of a decade of drought in the central portions of the prairies, combined with depressed grain prices (owing to a glut on the world market) and the 1929-30 Depression ushered in a period of economic instability. For many prairie service centres, the imperative was not one of handling the problems of growth, but one of how to weather the hardships and survive (Artibise, 1979).

The period 1930-1970

These hardships interrupted the region's agricultural development and, after 1930, initiated a period of uncertainty for the many trading centres whose viability was dependent on servicing farm populations. Settlements that were especially hard hit were those in the semi-arid areas of southern Saskatchewan and southeastern Alberta where the abandonment of wheat-producing farms was widespread (Schlichtmann, 1977). These adjustments in farming altered the density of farmstead settlement, farm sizes and occasionally the nature of farm production. Accordingly, the number of attendant service centres (with less than 1000 inhabitants) underwent a slight decline in Saskatchewan, but their numbers were more or less static in the adjoining two provinces (Table 1.3) whose fortunes were more influenced by the stagnant economy than by the prolonged drought. That the number of farmers and area of farmland actually increased throughout this period (Table 1.1) reflects the impact of government-sponsored schemes both to resettle farmers from drought-stricken areas and to engage the urban unemployed in mixed farming activities along the northern frontier of agriculture.

The widespread introduction of machinery was curtailed, however, by the financial hardships of the 1930s and later by World War II.[3] Although the replacement of men and draught animals gathered momentum after 1941, the rate of change increased dramatically after 1946 and substantially influenced the character and efficiency of prairie farms. This transition rebounded upon the network of service centres, and, in particular, jeopardized the viability of the lowest-order centres. Intra-regional differences in these changes were evident, as exemplified in grain-producing areas where farm consolidation was most pronounced and regarded as a necessary corollary of mechanization (Royal Commission Report, 1956). As a consequence of the greater use of machines, farm enlargement and the accruing economies of scale, the forces of economic Darwinism inexorably eliminated farms that were small and/or inefficient. Thus, with increases in tractor power and the capabilities of agricultural equipment, farm sizes have consistently grown with each intercensal decade since 1921, and, particularly, since 1951 (Table 1.4). In 1941 the number of prairie farms peaked at 296,400, and by 1971 had declined to 174,700, or by 41% (Table 1.1). The proportional loss of farm population was even greater, although its extent cannot be determined because the 1941 census did not divide the rural population into its non-farm and farm components. Nevertheless, between 1951 and 1971 the farm population declined by 37% from 952,669 to 599,770.

Another stimulus to rural change during this period was the improved system of transportation deriving from developments in road construction and the increased use of automobiles and trucks. The net result was that it reduced "the

---

[3] Leir (1971) describes the process of farm mechanization in the spring-wheat belt of Saskatchewan.

Table 1.4 Prairie Region: Changes in Mean Farm Size 1921-1981

Census Year	1921	1931	1941	1951	1961	1971	1981
	Mean Farm Size in Hectares						
Manitoba	111	113	118	137	170	220	259
Saskatchewan	194	164	175	223	278	342	385
Alberta	143	162	176	213	261	320	330
Prairie Region	139	154	164	202	250	309	347

Source: 1921 Census of Canada
1936 Census of Prairie Provinces
1961 Census of Canada
1981 Agricultural Censuses of Manitoba, Saskatchewan and Alberta

effective distance between rural farmsteads and the small towns ... [and] even more dramatically shortened those effective distances between rural farmsteads and the large towns and cities" (Dale, 1977). Smaller-sized centres, with their limited number of services, were increasingly bypassed as the source of local supplies and a depot for surplus farm produce. With motor vehicles assuming a greater role in local transportation, railways lost some of their significance as services were reduced and by the 1960s some were abandoned (Zimmerman and Moneo, 1971).

It has been deduced that as a result of agrarian and transportation changes small towns would be destined for extinction. However, such predictions were based on short-term trends and/or specific situations where small centres were declining in number. Furthermore, the fact was overlooked that over the longer term small towns and villages could alter the nature of their service roles and/or attract new economic activities in order to survive[4]. Evidence of this survival is provided by Table 1.3. For instance, in 1931 there were 415 trading centres in the region, of which 81% were lower-order centres with populations of less than 1000, whereas in 1971 the number of centres had increased to 575, with 70% being categorized as lower order. In this respect, however, Manitoba differs in that it exhibits stability; for example, 64% of its 55 trading centres in 1931 had low-order status, while 40 years later 63% of 79 centres were so classified.

Conclusion

Small towns remain an integral and vital part of the rural prairie scene. However, in view of the substantial decline in farm numbers that persisted throughout the 1960s and 1970s (Table 1.1), the long-term future of many of the smaller towns is veiled in uncertainty. It is in this context that an investigation is conducted of rural communities in the farming region of Manitoba for the 1971-1981 period. Here study can be made of settlements with traditional agrarian roots that remain largely untrammeled by other forms of economic development. In setting the stage for the analysis presented in Chapters 3 and 4, the following

---

[4] Fuguitt (1972) has noted that the assumed demise of small towns "ignores the possibility that small places may grow to become big ones and vice versa ....Thus in aggregate terms, the declining importance of small places may be due to their growth rather than their demise, along with a decline in the number of new places, as the settlement structure becomes established."

chapter introduces the region and reviews the economic and political developments pertinent to an appreciation of the study.

Chapter 2

Agro-Manitoba and Its Small Towns Prior to 1971

The Study Region and Farming Trends During the 1960s

As it implies, Agro-Manitoba is the southern part of the province in which agricultural activities are possible. This region has an area of 14.2 million ha and in 1971 had a population of 923,162 (93% of the provincial total). Winnipeg was home to 540,262 residents; 17 times the size of the second-ranking centre, Brandon (Figure 2.1).

Although Manitoba's economy had diversified since the 1940s, agriculture remained the pre-eminent activity throughout the 1960s. However, the intercensal decade 1961-71 was distinguished by an intensity of change affecting the farm sector that was relatively greater than the changes associated with the drought years of "The Dirty Thirties." Indeed, during the 1960s farm numbers declined by 19.2% to 34,981 and farm population dropped by 24.1% to 131,202. Concurrently, average farm size increased by 29.3% to 220 ha. All the 112 agricultural census subdivisions comprising Agro-Manitoba experienced a loss of farms (Figure 2.2). Rates of change in farm numbers differed according to the type of farming system, scale of enterprise, level of farm sales and the religious-ethnic identity of farmers (see Todd and Brierley, 1977; Brierley and Todd, 1978; and Todd, 1979).

With the loss of almost one out of every five farms in the 1960s, concern was expressed as to the future of the region's smaller communities. Their fundamental role of servicing rural farm families and marketing of the grain and

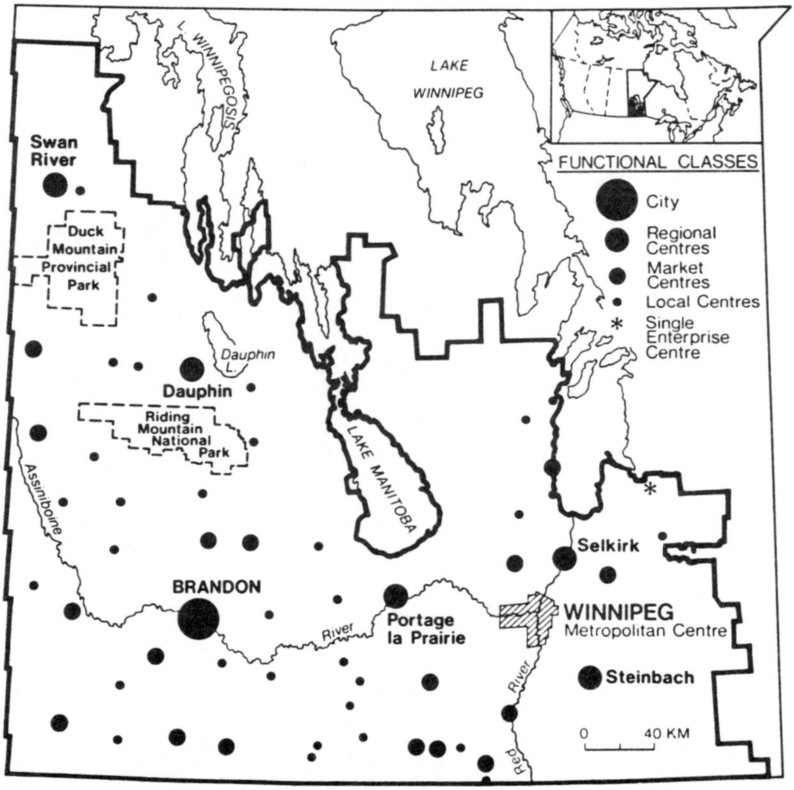

Figure 2.1 Agro-Manitoba: Functional Classification of Service Centres.

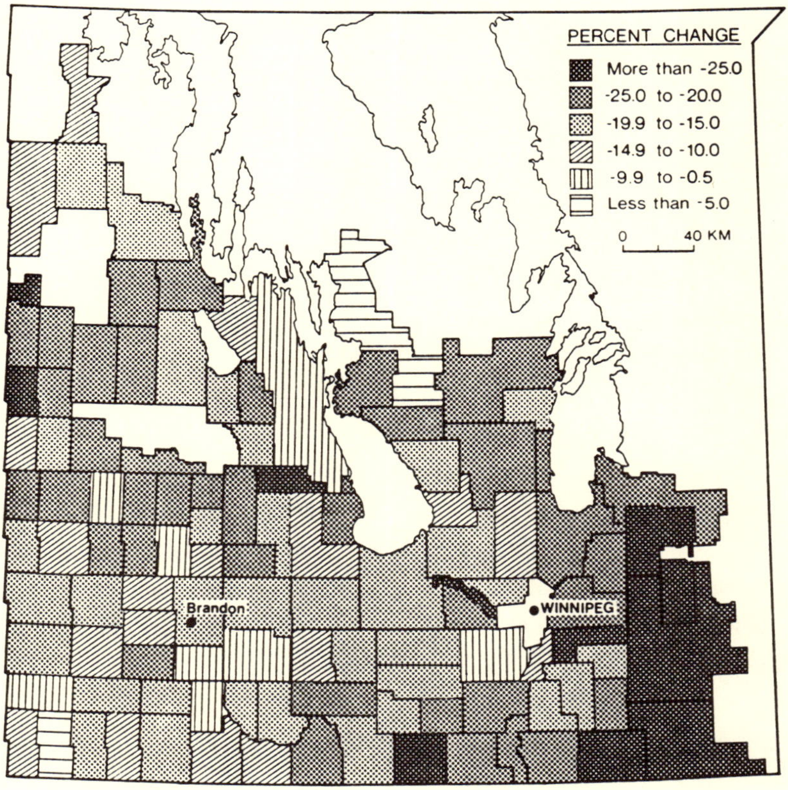

Figure 2.2 Agro-Manitoba: Percentage Change in Number of Farms by Census Subdivision 1961-1971.

livestock produced by those families was being called into question. Furthermore, for the first time since the commencement of agricultural settlement, the impact of declining farm numbers rebounded upon the rural non-farm population, which registered a loss of almost 3% between 1961 and 1966 (Report of the Commission on Targets for Economic Development, 1969).

Small Towns in 1971

In light of these agricultural adjustments some of the 58 small towns targeted in this study seemed to be facing bleak prospects.[1] Nevertheless, their combined population for 1971 stood at 133,269, 9.3% higher than that for 1961. In comparison, provincial growth for this period was 7.2%, largely the result of Winnipeg's population size increasing by 13.5%. To appreciate the nature of these changes, community size is relevant (Table 2.1 and Figure 2.3). Centres which contained at least 1000 inhabitants in 1961 were likely to have experienced population growth, whereas those of smaller size exhibited a mixed pattern of change. Of the 32 centres in the latter category, 9 had intercensal losses exceeding 5%, 12 remained essentially unchanged (between ± 5%), while the remainder had gains greater than 5%. Although certain towns were struggling to maintain their population base, the overall trend was one of small increase; a result which appears to refute a commonly held notion of the time that by rights the majority of these centres ought to be in a state of demise. However, there was a net loss of people in the 20 to 44 year age category (see Zimmerman and Moneo, 1971) resulting in an increase in the dependent components of the population.

Reaction by Provincial and Federal Governments

Even prior to the publication of the 1971 census, government departments had been alerted to the consequences that declining farm numbers could have on rural areas, and in the early 1960s both federal and provincial governments undertook for the first time comprehensive regional planning to mitigate the

---

[1] The term 'small towns' in this study incorporates urban communities whose population size ranged from 450 to more than 30,000 in 1971. Smaller-sized centres, such as hamlets and villages, are excluded from analysis because they are not generally included in provincial statistics and, thus, lack data coverage.

Table 2.1 Agro-Manitoba: Population Trends 1961-1971 by Size Category of Small Town

	Population Trends 1961-1971 number of centres			
Size category of small town	Declined <5%	Stagnant -5 to +5%	Increased >5%	% Total Population Change
<1000 residents	9	12	11	5.2
1000-3400 residents	3	4	14	9.2
>3400 residents	-	1	4	12.1
Total	12	17	29	9.3

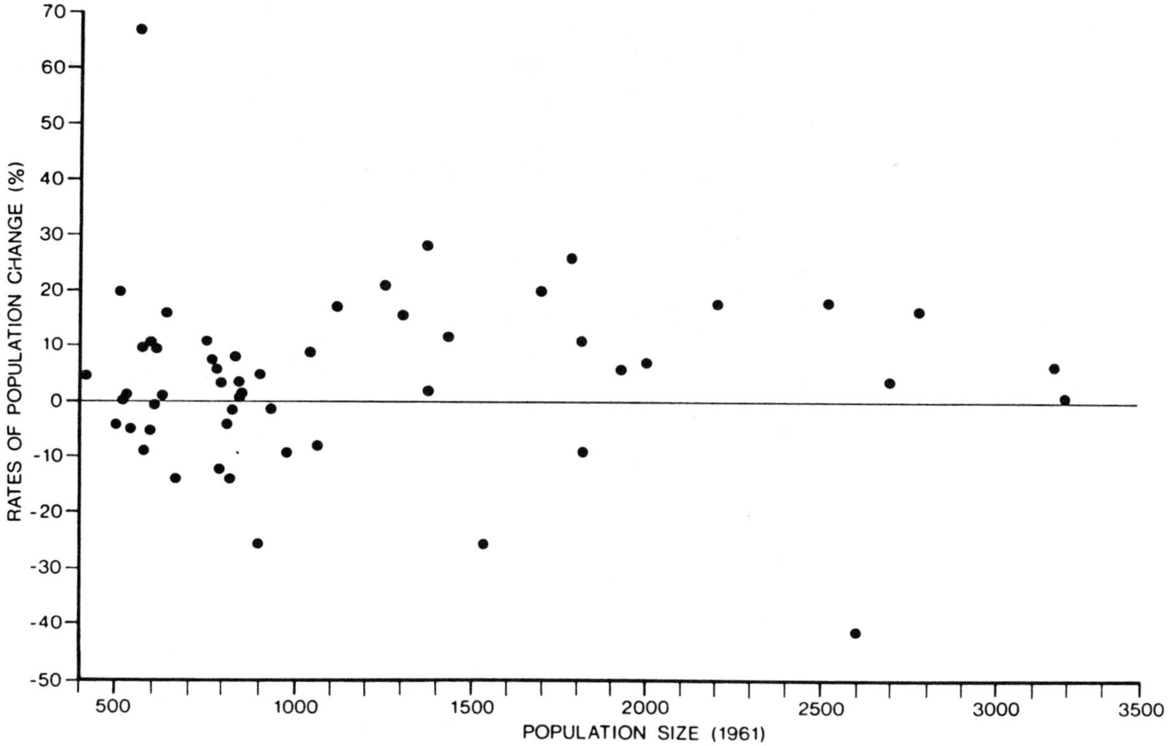

Figure 2.3 Agro-Manitoba: Rates of Population Change 1961-1971 by Population Size of Small Towns With Less Than 3,400 Residents.

degree and extent of intra-provincial disparities. At the provincial level, there were essentially three initiatives; two associated with an administration headed by Progressive Conservatives and the other with that of the New Democratic Party. The former embrace the reports of the Committee on Manitoba's Economic Future (COMEF) and the Commission on Targets for Economic Development (TED), while the latter was responsible for a policy blueprint entitled *Guidelines for the Seventies*. Federal government involvement was generally undertaken through joint federal-provincial ventures, including the Agricultural and Rural Development Act, the Fund for Rural Economic Development and the Small Farm Development Program.

The COMEF report of 1963 was a planning document "developed in response to forces such as technological change that were rearranging the economy of the province" (Sarbit and Greer-Wootten, 1980). Its aim was to determine the means by which an additional 40,000 jobs could be created within the province by 1970. It was particularly concerned with stemming emigration from Manitoba of skilled and educated members of the labour force. However, the report recognized that farm consolidation was "not necessarily" detrimental, as it resulted in more efficient farms and, furthermore, that the implications of such losses should not be left to chance with local community initiatives being encouraged to ensure development through rural industrialization and the expansion of educational, commercial and recreational facilities (COMEF, 1963). An inherent problem of this report was that it did not specify the source of financial support for these improvements (Sarbit and Greer-Wootten, 1980). Such an oversight was indicative of others that plagued preliminary provincial efforts at regional planning and resulted in the report being ineffective since it left local communities to 'their own devices' and in competition with each other. Tacit acknowledgement of COMEF's failure came in 1966 when the Progressive Conservatives established another commission, TED, with similar objectives to those of COMEF.

The Report of TED, released in 1969, provides insights into Progressive Conservative philosophy regarding economic development. One of its principal differences from COMEF is in the emphasis TED placed on reducing long-standing regional disparities. As denoted by its title, the TED Report provided "numerical targets" which were considered to be the basis for "balanced regional development"

(TED, 1969). The Report acknowledged that residents of Agro-Manitoba, other than those in Winnipeg and Brandon, were faced with problems induced by technological change and

> ... regardless of what course of action is chosen, Manitoba's farm population will continue to shrink and the smaller rural centres will continue to disappear.... By 1980, it is conceivable that there will be 20,000 farms, as opposed to roughly 37,000 at present and that there will be fewer than 40 agricultural centres in Manitoba's rural regions compared to more than 60 at present (TED, 1969).[2]

Such an outcome for the farm sector indicated a "laissez-faire" attitude on the part of the Conservatives and an unwillingness to arrest the forces of economic Darwinism in agricultural circles. Hence, the decay of the smallest service centres was "inevitable."

With the assumption of power by the New Democratic Party in 1969, a socialistic stamp was placed on Manitoba's development strategies that are detailed in their *Guidelines for the Seventies*. Four principles underscored this planning document, namely:

i) maximization of the well-being of all Manitobans;

ii) greater equality for all provincial residents achieved through an equitable distribution of benefits obtained from development;

iii) implementation of policies and programmes for an effective 'stay option'; which would allow Manitobans to remain in that part of the province where they desired to live; and

iv) promotion of public participation in government (*Guidelines for the Seventies*, 1973).

Rural areas, especially, stood to benefit from the 'stay option' which represented an attempt to check out-migration arising from rural disadvantages. For Agro-Manitoba, a revitalized agricultural sector was deemed the means by which farmers would remain on the land. To this end, the Guidelines provided specific objectives for agriculture. First, it advocated increased farm output in order to raise total

[2] In fact the 1981 Agricultural Census recorded 29,442 farms.

through diversification of farm production and improvements in marketing and stability in capital costs which were to derive from central purchasing of farm supplies. Thirdly, the viability of low- and middle-income producers was to be enhanced by programmes directed at providing small- and medium-scale farmers with financial and management assistance (*Guidelines for the Seventies,* 1973). In order to put in practice the 'stay option' and the participation principles, the New Democrats emphasized decentralization of provincial government services throughout rural Manitoba. For farmers, this meant that most should be situated no more than 30-minutes travelling time from a Department of Agriculture centre. Similarly, facilities for health care, basic social services and education were to be readily accessible.

Concurrent with the provincially-induced initiatives, joint federal-provincial undertakings focussed on more specific rural problems. The first of note was the Agricultural Rehabilitation and Development Act (ARDA) of 1961, which stemmed from the realization that the level of income and standard of living of many rural people were sufficiently low as to require government action (Giles, 1978). Initially ARDA supported projects that would intensify farm production, raise farm income and increase the level of living and opportunities of rural inhabitants. Emphasis was placed on research, issues of land use, farm adjustment, soil and water conservation, and general rural development, but by 1965, with the second ARDA (renamed Agricultural and Rural Development Act in 1966) agreement, the list of project categories was expanded to include training and public information services, together with the formation of rural development and special rural development areas. In 1971, the third ARDA agreement emphasized improving farm income by diversifying production from grain to livestock, with preference being given to farmers with gross sales between $5000 and $15,000 (Ward, 1977).

Additionally, the Fund for Rural Economic Development (FRED), set up by the federal government in 1966, provided new thrusts in regional economic development via comprehensive federal-provincial agreements. FRED was specifically targeted at regions suffering from social and economic depression and was to assume responsibility for ARDA's special rural development areas, such as Manitoba's Interlake region situated between lakes Winnipeg and Manitoba. In

1967 FRED set aside a total of $85 million to stimulate the Interlake's economy over a ten-year period through:

i) improved educational facilities;

ii) establishment of vocational training facilities;

iii) development of the economic potential of the renewable resource sector, including farming and fishing;

iv) industrial development and;

v) development of the region's infrastructure by improving roads, housing and recreational facilities, which would provide added employment and raise the standard of living (Canada/Manitoba, n.d., p. 29).

Agricultural projects were prominent, especially those geared to establishing viable farms specializing in pasture and forage crops supporting beef cattle.

Another federal government initiative was the Small Farm Development Programs (SFDP) of 1971. This federal-provincial agreement was an attempt to retard the loss of small farms through the provision of special credit facilities and management and development services (Ward, 1977), thereby endorsing the 'stay option.'

In order for the 'stay option' to be effectively implemented, the New Democratic provincial government identified the need for a comprehensive assessment of existing social and economic conditions in the various urban communities within Southern Manitoba. Such information would provide the basis by which private and government investment could be channelled into selected growth centres. In 1971 a planning group within the provincial department of Industry and Commerce was charged with the responsibility of formulating a Regional Analysis Program (RAP) for Southern Manitoba. RAP amassed a detailed inventory of both objective and subjective indicators of conditions as they existed in 1971 for the region's small towns, providing us with an array of variables that are invaluable to the subsequent analysis of the 58 small towns (see Appendix 2.1 for 'objective' criteria).

Of particular significance to this study are the subjective measures that RAP gathered in 1971. These were obtained from a questionnaire survey of a 5% sample of households in Southern Manitoba. This survey provided indicators of community satisfaction and involvement by gauging the respondent's perceptions and preferences on a range of issues, such as shopping patterns, availability and quality of medical facilities, levels of satisfaction with respect to the local social milieu and leadership, views on the prospects for the town and the degree of participation in community affairs.[3] An appreciation of these subjective, quality-of-life indicators was deemed by RAP to be of crucial importance for the implementing of policies that would support an effective 'stay option.'

Functional Classification of Towns for 1971

One outcome of RAP was a functional classification of the region's small towns into city, regional centre, market centre, local centre and single-enterprise centre categories depending on central-place attributes (RAP, Working Paper No. 2, 1974). Figure 2.1 shows the distribution of our targeted 58 communities in Agro-Manitoba according to this four-fold system.

Excluding Winnipeg, the sole community in Agro-Manitoba possessing in 1971 the functional attributes of a city was Brandon. Its population size for that date was 31,150, an increase of 10.6% over the preceding decade. Besides possessing a community college and university, Brandon's economy was characterized by a diversity of service and trade industries, a relatively strong manufacturing sector and 28% of the region's provincial civil service employment.

Of secondary importance in the functional hierarchy are the regional centres of Dauphin, Portage la Prairie, Selkirk, Steinbach and Swan River (Figure 2.1). These centres, whose average size was about 8000 persons in 1971, were the most vibrant category at this time, as they collectively had experienced growth of 13.2% since 1961. For their economic underpinnings, these centres relied mainly on the provision of trade, business, community and personal services.

RAP identified 17 market centres, whose average size was 2100 persons and overall rate of growth for the preceding decade was 11.3%. Only one centre in this category had registered a decline in population for the 1961-71 period. These communities had a moderate degree of economic diversity in trade, business,

---

[3] Details of the questionnaire and its findings are contained in *Update, Volume One, Part 1A, Descriptive Data Regional Development Program Southern Manitoba,* Department of Industry and Commerce, Winnipeg, 1975.

community and personal services. Nevertheless, they had received a larger than proportional share of the region's recently-created manufacturing jobs (RAP, Working Paper No. 2) and were regarded as having buoyant economies. In addition, they appear to have consolidated their trade and service roles during the 1960s largely at the expense of local centres (RAP, Working Paper No. 1); the most numerous of all categories of communities, numbering 34. These centres had population sizes ranging from 480 to 1300 persons in 1971. As their population had increased only by 0.9% since 1961, their economic fortunes exhibited considerable variation. The most dramatic decline was associated with what had been the largest local centre in 1961, Rivers, which, owing to the closure of an air base had declined in size by 25.3%. On the other hand, a couple of centres had gains greater than 20%, largely because they had attracted new industry. But for the most part, these local centres bore the brunt of the impact resulting from declining farm numbers, and with economic development bypassing them the result was the out-migration of people in the working-age cohorts and an aging of their populations.

Summary and Conclusion

Notwithstanding the substantial reduction in the number of farms and associated farm population that occurred in Agro-Manitoba during the 1960s, small towns generally managed to weather the resulting social and economic consequences. Most exhibited a tenacity to survive, although concern was expressed for the future of local centres, since their economic underpinnings had been drastically weakened. Nevertheless, these centres defied the odds and maintained their population base even though the lack of rural employment opportunities prompted the out-migration of those mainly in the youthful age categories. Governments, both federal and provincial, recognized the long-term implications of rural depopulation to be detrimental to the welfare of small communities. A variety of programmes were implemented to ameliorate the lot of small towns, principally through both farm assistance schemes and nonagrarian economic diversification strategies for rural communities. The impact that these programmes had upon the region's small towns is apparent in the subsequent analysis for the 1971-81 intercensal decade.

Chapter 3

Economic Underpinnings

The combination of factors affecting Agro-Manitoba in the 1970s appear to have had an ambivalent impact on the region's small towns. On the one hand, secular changes in agriculture imposing capital-intensive activities at the expense of labour tended to undermine the rural population base with commensurate dire implications for central-place servicing. On the other hand, restructured service provisions compounded by regional planning attempts at economic diversification served to bolster the socioeconomic fabric of those small towns. To further complicate matters the rapid aging of the rural population as a result of selective out-migration of the younger cohorts as well as natural longevity has imposed new service requirements on the small towns while, simultaneously, injecting a new burden of dependency. The object of this chapter is to unravel the economic underpinnings of the region's small towns in light of these demographic tendencies. It begins with a discussion of population change over the 1971-81 decade and its differential impact on the set of small towns. The varying degrees of demographic dependency so outlined constitute the backcloth for an exposition of the communities' economic base, the mainstay of the chapter.

Population change is assessed by means of shift-share analysis (SSA). The advantage of applying SSA is its ability to suggest the causes for the disparate record of rapidly growing, sluggish, stagnant and declining populations displayed by the various communities. It allows for a breakdown of the constituents of population into 'young' (up to 19 years), 'intermediate' (20 to 54 years) and 'old'

(55 and over) categories and pinpoints whether their respective performances in discrete settlements derived from 'structural' or 'residual' factors. Specifically, the components of SSA are demarcated as:

> **Total shift** for settlement i (TS_i) is the amount by which the particular cohort has grown or fallen short of the figure which it should have attained if it had performed exactly in proportion of its stature in the set as a whole at the beginning of the period of change.
>
> **Structural shift** for settlement i (SS_i) is that aspect of TS_i attributed to the settlement having a disproportionate allocation of fast-growing cohorts or slow-growing cohorts.
>
> **Residual shift** for settlement i (RS_i) is TS_i - SS_i or, that aspect of the total shift not ascribed to structural factors. Conventionally, it is taken as representing geographic influences, for example, the effects of isolation (imposing a tendency for $-RS_i$) and proximity to major metropolitan areas (imposing a boosting effect).

The disaggregation into age cohorts allows for interesting speculations to be made on the 'economic health' of communities. For example, those suffering negative shifts for the intermediate category are symptomatic of settlements newly experiencing a decline in their economic bases. Similarly, communities displaying negative young and intermediate categories in combination are expressive of more long-standing economic decline. Conversely, positive shifts for the older categories conform to what Hodge and Qadeer (1983) have called "truncated communities," or those that have, by and large, lost their economic rationale altogether. Equally apparent, those communities that have positive shifts for both their young and intermediate cohorts are tantamount to being vibrant communities, presumably well endowed with economic opportunities.

As is evident from Table 3.1, the majority of the settlements analysed actually lost population in the younger cohorts between 1971 and 1981, a state of affairs that underscores the fragile basis of communities with less than 1000 people throughout the Prairie economy. Of equal significance is the finding that population gain throughout the small-town sector is confined for the most part to

Table 3.1 Shift-Share Results

Characteristic	No. of settlements recording '+'	recording '-'
Absolute population		
growth - ('young')	9[1]	46
- ('intermediate')	44[2]	12
- ('old')	55	3
TS_i - 'young'	5	53
- 'intermediate'	13[3]	34
- 'old'	46	12

Notes: 1. Also three recording 'no change'
2. Also two recording 'no change'
3. Also one recording 'no change'

Table 3.2 Shift-Share Combinations

Combination of shifts for	'Young'	'Intermediate'	'Old'	Number of settlements
		-TS (+SS; -RS)		34
	-TS (-SS: -RS)			36
	-TS (-SS; +RS)			17
	-TS.............+.........	-TS		34
			+TS (+SS: +RS)	22
			+TS (+SS; -RS)	24
	-TS.............+..........	-TS.......+.........	+TS	26
	+TS (-SS: +RS)			5
		+TS (+SS; +RS)		16
		+TS (+SS: -RS)		6
	+TS............+........	+TS		5

the intermediate and old categories of person, a situation which does not offer much promise for the long-term future of these settlements. Consistent with absolute change is the outcome whereby positive total shifts are mainly associated with the older populations of the towns, whereas the young and intermediate categories are primarily exhibiting negative total shifts. Clearly, the majority of settlements are making disproportionate gains in the elderly, but less-than-proportionate gains in the young and intermediate populations. The 'truncated' nature of many settlements is further brought out in Table 3.2. No less than 26 of the 58 settlements are characterized by a state of negative total shifts for the young and intermediates combined with positive total shifts for the elderly. Such symptoms of decline merit clarification. Thus, of the 53 communities recording -TS for the young, two-thirds register -RS. As all 53 record negative structural shifts, the -RS implication is that isolation may account for much of the explanation inherent in poor performance. By the same token, all 34 of the settlements recording -TS for the intermediate population do so in combination with +SS and -RS characteristics. In other words, they are failing to maintain their share of an active labour force despite an above-average growth of the structurally-dominant sector (i.e., the older population cohorts) and, by virtue of their geographic isolation or other such impediment. On the plus side, a mere five settlements have gained disproportionate numbers of young and intermediates and that minority group represents the true 'growth' segment of the small-town sector in as much as it hints at economic dynamism with all that it entails in terms of job openings and the security of livelihood necessary to induce the formation of young families. A significantly larger number of communities record +TS for the intermediates but without the impetus to carry over into enhanced growth in the younger cohorts. These newly declining communities also display disproportionate growth in the elderly (i.e., the +SS) common to settlements as a whole, but are mostly the beneficiaries of +RS recordings (16 out of 22) which seems to put them within close proximity of Winnipeg and Brandon.

The above comments suffice to set the scene for the following discussion on economic issues. They have served to indicate that, first of all, the majority of communities in the region are 'truncated' by being endowed with a disproportionately large population of elderly people. Secondly, SSA implies that an increasing number of communities are failing to ensure ongoing demographic dynamism in that their younger age cohorts are drying up. Thirdly, the -RS factor appears to play a major role in the demographics of such problem communities, hinting at the prevalence of regional considerations (superficially, taken to mean the outcomes imposed by geographic isolation) in the effective operations of Prairie settlements. Finally, and notwithstanding the population turnaround phenomenon trumpeted elsewhere in North America, analysis underscores the fact that the number of communities actually expanding across the demographic age spectrum is both absolutely, as well as relatively, small in Agro-Manitoba.

Economic Activities

The Servicing Function

The formation of Prairie settlements owes much to the central-place role accorded them at the time of the opening up of the region. Consistent with the systematic spatial and functional patterns advocated by the Christaller school, many settlements were grain-collection points (elevator sites on the railway) combining some retailing function for the surrounding rural farm population. That said, it is unclear as to the extent that subsequent fortunes of these settlements have rested on this narrow central-place role. To argue, as Hodge (1965) has done, that smaller central places (villages) will disappear partly as a result of the vulnerability of their sparse offering of retail functions and partly in consequence of their being by-passed as shopping centres by a newly mobile rural farm population is at one and the same time intuitively reasonable but overly simplistic. Without doubt, enhanced personal transportation can disrupt established retail patterns, but its impact has probably been overestimated (Brunner and Lorge, 1973; Johansen and Fuguitt, 1984). Moreover, while it is true that the number of retail businesses in rural small towns has, in aggregate, tended to decline over the last two or more decades, that decline has afflicted all rural small towns in the central-place hierarchy of the Prairies irrespective of size (Zimmerman and Moneo, 1971). Rural consumers are not abandoning retailers in the smallest small towns for those in larger centres. Conceivably, businessmen in the smaller retail centres may have sought to counter decline by adopting some of the trappings of the so-called 'dispersed city.' Opting for specialization, the retailers of a number of adjoining villages and towns connive at a division of labour amongst themselves and are, in consequence, patronized by a mobile, dispersed population not only from the constituent set of settlements ('the dispersed city'), but from the surrounding farm population as well (Hart et al.,1968; Dahms, 1980).

So long as economic diversification remains elusive, settlements in Agro-Manitoba will stand or fall to a significant extent on their ability to provide the functions assigned to them by agriculture. This dependence is best envisaged by way of a variation on the cumulative causation concept (Todd, 1983a). Since World War II, as increased mechanization in agriculture has led directly to farm consolidation, labour replacement, and the abandonment of rural areas by displaced farmers and farm workers alike, rural small towns have lost much of the consumer market which formerly propped up their commercial activities (Wallace and Drudy, 1973). If the level of patronage falls below a certain critical mass (the threshold of central-place theory), then the retail establishment will flounder. Release of labour from small-town businesses only exacerbates declining retail volumes and may induce a domino effect on other businesses. Should the disappearance of demand continue unchecked, then the community is in danger of losing its viability as a provider of economic opportunities. While Prairie agriculture has undergone the secular process of mechanization, the side-effects of that process have rarely impacted on small-town fortunes to the extent of forcing the dissolution of entire communities. In other words, negative cumulative causation is not taken to its logical conclusion because of the offsetting influences of public services on the one hand (especially health care and housing) and diversified economic activities (manufacturing) on the other.

Manufacturing

Manufacturing has always been present in small-towns, at least that branch of manufacturing concerned with agricultural processing. The traditional characteristics of bulkiness and perishability were powerful factors in inducing village-level manufacturing. It has formed the semblance of an industrial sector throughout the Prairie settlement system for many years. Table 3.3 confirms the fact that over the 1962-75 period, the vast bulk of manufacturing activities found in

Table 3.3 Characteristic Manufacturing Activities found in Prairie Non-Metropolitan Centres, 1962-1975

Community size (and number)	Industry	Average size (in employment)
Below 1000 population (92)	Feed	<25
	Agricultural Implements	25-99
	Inorganic Industrial Chemicals	100
	Fish Products	<25
1000-2499 (49)	Agricultural Implements	100
	Miscellaneous Machinery	25-99
	Miscellaneous Food Processors	25-99
	Plastics	25-99
2500-4999 (26)	Soft Drinks	<25
	Petroleum Refining	25-99
	Vegetable Oil	25-99
	Publishing and Printing	<25
	Agricultural Implements	25-99
5000-7499 (9)	Soft Drinks	<25
	Structural Concrete	<25
7500-9999 (4)	Soft Drinks	25-99
	Pre-fabricated Buildings	100
10,000-19,999 (4)	Soft Drinks	<25
	Agricultural Implements	<25
	Sash and Door Plants	<25
20,000-49,999 (5)	Soft Drinks	25-99
	Structural Concrete	25-99
	Machine Shops	<25
	Agricultural Implements	25-99
	Clay Products	25-99

Source: Todd (1977)

non-metropolitan centres across the three Prairie Provinces was either directly associated with agricultural and other resource processing or indirectly linked with it by way of fulfilling the specialist needs of the farm sector (i.e., agricultural implements production and machine shops). The table also demonstrates that they are widely dispersed throughout the small-town system. Manufacturing of this nature should not be disparaged because it enhances the per capita income of settlements as well as providing job openings (Rogers et al., 1978). It does not, however, remove the potential instability of an economy of a community which remains reliant on an agricultural (or other resource) base.

In Manitoba, however, manufacturing is something of a weak reed. While it is true to say that it accounted for virtually all of the growth in output, employment and investment which occurred in the province in the 1970s, it is equally true that the force of the growth was insufficient to prevent a net loss of interprovincial migrants (MSERD, 1984). For industries unconnected with the agricultural base, there exist a number of constraints on expansion in Manitoba. In particular, the limited local market and its corollary of substantial distances to other larger markets have worked against enterprise formation in the region. Fortunately, the abundance of cheap electrical energy (a product of the hydroelectric generating facilities in northern Manitoba) in conjunction with readily available (and moderately priced) labour offer some inducements to firms willing to forgo metropolitan locations and transfer their plants to the province's small towns. While these assets are currently more latent than real, the province's small towns have thrown up a smattering of local entrepreneurs who have chosen to establish their firms in situ rather than heading for the city. A survey of the clothing and transportation equipment industries drew the conclusion that, "By far the most important reasons given for starting up a firm in Manitoba involve personal *nonbusiness* factors. Generally this response seems to mean that those starting the firms lived in Manitoba and saw no reason to pull up roots and move elsewhere before setting up business" (Economic Council of Canada, 1984). It follows, then, that the region has a tradition of producing home-grown manufacturing enterprise and, in addition, has a good chance of retaining that enterprise.

The formation of manufacturing in small towns is certainly a worthwhile exercise in so far as job creation is concerned. After an exhaustive review of the

U.S. situation, Summers et al., (1976) conclude that those communities receiving plants invariably boost their populations as a result. Moreover, population growth is a function of the stature of the industrial enterprise and is likely to follow from induced in-migration to the community. New migrants will, for the most part, derive from the area adjacent to the community. The labour effects are industry specific, that is to say, low-skill, low-wage, female-oriented employment is mainly the preserve of clothing, textile and electronics-assembly plants, whereas better-paying male-oriented jobs occur in heavy industries. A knock-on effect, however, is the straining of community service delivery systems.

Manufacturers appear to have various preferences when choosing plant locations in small towns. One of the most persistent is their desire to locate within reasonable proximity of metropolitan centres, partly because these are minimum-distance moves away from the centres which originally spawned the businesses and, partly, owing to the continued need of businesses to have access to the infrastructure available in cities. As Averitt (1979) notes, the first reason alludes to the traditional role of cities, that of seedbeds of industrial development, and allows for a life cycle where at a subsequent stage of evolution industries may become sufficiently footloose to forsake metropolitan sites for small-town alternatives (see also Lonsdale and Seyler, 1979). The second reason is perhaps best endorsed through an actual example. One of North America's biggest manufacturers of cable television parts decided to build a plant at Stonewall, a town about 30-minutes drive from Winnipeg, in order to share the community's 'small-town atmosphere' while, at one and the same time, having easy access to Winnipeg International Airport.

Proximity to metropolitan areas also hints at the attenuation of agglomeration economies. Hansen (1974) has noted that industries capable of long-term survival in small towns are, by virtue of their exclusion from cities, largely indifferent to agglomeration economies. Instead, they rely on attractively priced labour or make use of extensive amounts of land for storage and waste disposal. Characteristically, the newly locating rural industries are of small size and utilize standardized production methods. They are concerned with minimizing competition for labour and are aided in this respect by choosing dispersed locations (Erickson, 1974). One study concluded that the rural industrializing trend is attributable to the desire of firms to "(1)... move or locate far enough away from their own existing plants to maintain a non-union plant or at least to escape the jurisdiction of their current union and (2) to move out of the orbit of their competitors for labour" (Stafford, 1974).

In moving from the general to the particular, an attempt at inferring the determinants of Prairie manufacturing arrived at some illuminating findings (Todd, 1977). Using a sample of 170 settlements of 1000 population and above, a multiple regression analysis was conducted with manufacturing employment per town in 1976 as the dependent variable (see Table 3.4). The analysis suggests that manufacturing employment is positively associated with size of settlement and its corollaries of expanding markets as well as larger labour forces and a pre-existing industrial presence. The inverse relationships point to deficiencies in those markets (i.e., the larger market centres are 'importing' their consumer goods rather than being self-sufficient in manufactures) on the one hand, and a discrepancy between industrialization and the provision of social infrastructure on the other. What is more, the negative relationship with primary employment implies that manufacturing tends to steer clear of agriculturally oriented settlements.

A Small-Town Economic Model

The three themes underscoring the functional role of Prairie settlements, the continuing importance of the agricultural base, the adaptation of service activities and the hosting of secondary manufacturing, all need to be drawn together in a formal way such that the relative importance and interdependence of these themes can be established.

A point of departure for the model is the assumption that Prairie settlements continue, by and large, to function as service centres with a fundamental dependence between population size and servicing role. That relationship, however, merely masks another and more basic one, which is, the dependence of services on a population that is itself dependent upon the level of agricultural activity. From a commercial standpoint, services rise and fall according to fluctuations in man:land ratios in the surrounding rural areas. The only exceptions to this rule of thumb are, first, that rising income levels among the farm community may compensate for declining numbers of farmers among them (to a degree unspecified), secondly, that services may progressively lose their dependence on rural customers if the town can stimulate its own industrial development and conjure up an alternative urban clientele and, finally, that those services may become public operations with a mandate for providing social facilities regardless of commercial considerations.

The first point is self evident - the failure of many small service centres to disappear, as so often predicted, leads to the conclusion that smaller rural populations can support a continuing range of services in small towns as a direct result of their enhanced per capita incomes. Yet this assertion can only be taken so far. Farm consolidation and mechanization ultimately reduce the farm population to such an extent that for all the survivors' wealth, there is an insufficient basis of demand to support a range of business in the adjacent small towns. Only by removing the dependence of town services on the custom of farm families is the vicious circle avoided. Economic diversification by means of manufacturing provides an alternative basis of demand for small-town services. Not only does manufacturing create direct jobs but, as a consequence of the multiplier process, indirect and induced jobs in the service sector as well. In combination, the new jobs encourage younger people to stay in small towns, garner younger people from surrounding farms and hamlets and thereby mitigate the tendency towards population truncation. Paradoxically, manufacturing may opt for those communities enjoying a good endowment of services in the first place. Thus, while the level of service activity may be boosted by the presence of manufacturing, it is equally true that manufacturing may be dependent on the location of services for its regional distribution.

Figure 3.1 drafts out the relationships inherent in the model. The fundamental relationships as outlined are supplemented by three other concerns. In the first place, due allowance is made for the partial dependence of manufacturing on the agricultural base (which is to say, those industrial processes which transform agrarian products). Secondly, a number of factors are included in order to account for the formation of other types of manufacturing in the rural small towns. Thirdly, the effect of subjective factors expressed through quality-of-life indicators needs to be acknowledged. As man 'does not live by bread alone,' the existence of

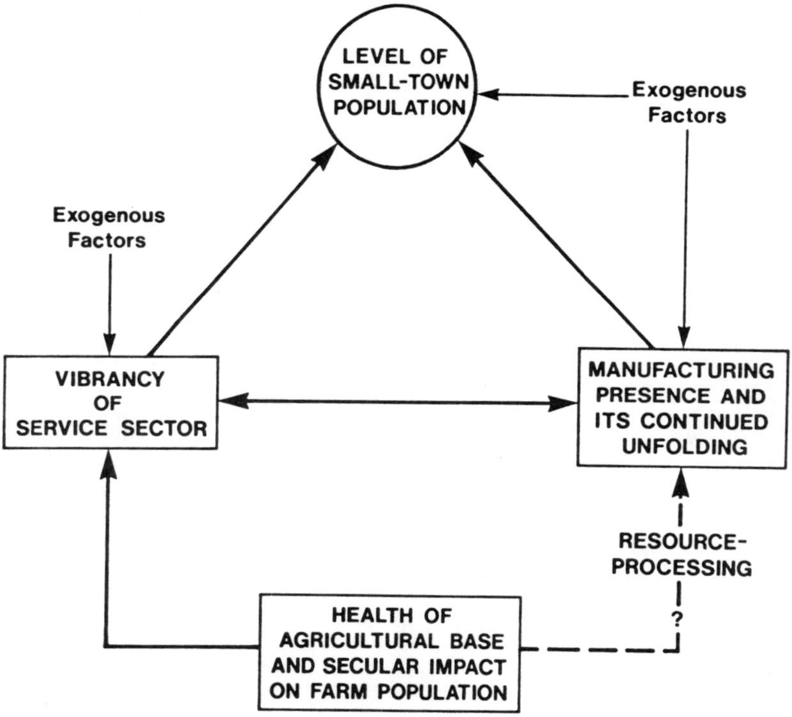

Figure 3.1 The Economic Model.

Table 3.4 Determinants of Prairie Manufacturing Employment

Variable[1]	Regression Coefficient	Statistical Significance
Population potential[2]	.034	.01
Market potential[2]	-.034	.01
Number of plants	.310	.01
Number of detached homes	1.022	.01
Number of hospital beds	-.111	.01
1971 population	.813	.05
1976 population	-.564	.01
Primary employment	-.046	.01
Taxable income	.390	.05

1. Dependent variable is manufacturing employment in each of 170 settlements drawn from Alberta, Saskatchewan and Manitoba.

2. Population potential is defined as: Σ_j (P/d)
and Market potential is: Σ_j(M/d)
where 'P' is town population, 'M' is aggregate income of the town, and 'd" is distance between 'i' and 'j' where j=1.... 170.

intangible factors boosting the welfare of small-town residents may play a significant part in preventing further population erosion. To accommodate these concerns, the model adopts a multiple-equation format in which each equation has a dependent variable (in turn, population change between 1971 and 1981, level of service employment 1981, and level of manufacturing employment 1981) and a number of determinants. Some of the determinants are common to two equations and the dependent variables also act as determinants in equations other than their own. The agricultural key determinant does not warrant its own equation because it acts, in the form of primary employment change, as an exogenous (given) influence on both level of service employment and level of manufacturing employment.

The establishment of a model consisting of an equation system which contains endogenous variables (i.e., those that are 'determined' by the system in the first place, and constitute determinants elsewhere in the system in the second) obviously requires a regression solution geared to handling simultaneity bias. For that purpose, the two-stage least squares (2SLS) procedure is resorted to. In similar fashion to the classical multiple regression (ordinary least squares), 2SLS estimates each equation separately but unlike OLS, it is capable of accommodating endogenous and exogenous variables. In other words, it can deal with the interdependence between services and manufacturing in the context of our small-town system. Assuming that the order conditions of the equations are met (which they are in our model), then each equation can be identified and its regression coefficients are meaningful. A note of caution needs sounding, however, in that the usual significance tests (t and F) are invalid with 2SLS owing to their unknown distributions (Pindyck and Rubinfeld, 1976). It is admissible, however, to maintain that the unknown distributions are asymptotically normal with samples of comparable size to ours, and such is the stance adopted herein for hypothesis testing.

Model specification is evinced through Table 3.5 (Appendix 3.1 defines the variables). Equation 1 elicits the influences on population change underway in the 58 Manitoba communities between 1971 and 1981. Above all, it highlights the dependence of small-town population upon the two endogenous variables representing levels of service and manufacturing. As is evident from the standardized regression coefficients (ßs), only the latter has a significant impact on population even though both of them behave in the anticipated direct manner. Very emphatically, therefore, the preeminence of manufacturing as a determinant of Manitoban small-town population growth is in full accord with the overall North American experience (Roepke and Freudenberg, 1981), and this is so despite the history of relatively sparse industrialization in the Prairies. The most significant regressors, however, are the total shift for the young age category on the one hand and V8 - a subjective indicator - on the other. The latter needs some elaboration. In view of the diverse means of monitoring community satisfaction and the wealth of material accumulated (recall Chapter 2), indicators of quality-of-life required for insertion into the 2SLS need to be refined. This course is expedient not only for the purpose of clarification, but also to reduce the interaction (multicollinearity) inherent in many of the subjective variables. Following Warren's (1963) precedent, ten quality-of-life indicators for Manitoban small towns are derived (Table 3.6). The first three (S_1-S_3) reflect feelings about local systems of production, distribution and consumption, two each are expressions of social support (S_4-S_5), socialization (S_6-S_7) and social participation (S_8-S_9), whereas the final indicator (S_{10}) is a measure of social control. These subjective variables are subjected to principal components analysis in order to summarize their content and produce orthogonal variables for the regression model. Three components emerge with a cumulative variance of 85% and they can be labelled as a socialization dimension (V8 on Table 3.6), a production/consumption dimension (V9), and a dichotomized low-order retail or health-care dimension (V10). The socialization dimension accounts for by far the largest amount of total variance and, indeed, it is the only subjective component to emerge as a significant regressor in Equation 1. Its high level of significance implies that it is positively related to recent population change among the towns and villages. It follows, therefore, that expanding towns have residents who are satisfied with their community, think that it has a future, and are actively involved in its affairs. The TS 'young' coefficient, meanwhile, implies that those communities gaining a disproportionate share of the under-19s are likely to be in the vanguard of overall population gain. As a supplement, the communities experiencing gain in the previous decade (as indicated via V13) are likely to build on those gains in the subsequent years: a 'success breeds success' phenomenon. The

Table 3.5 Model Specification and Results (Betas)

Variable	Equation 1 (Y = V21)	Equation 2 (Y = V11)	Equation 3 (Y = V21)
1981 Health Index (V1)	-.062		
1981 Education Index (V2)	-.010		
1981 Transport Infrastructure (V3)	-.243*		
1980 Average Income (V4)	-.060		
1981 % Unemployment (V5)	-.245*		
1971-81 TS 'Young' (V6)	.432**		
Metropolitan Proximity (V7)	.021		-.147*
lst Subjective Component (V8)	.413**	-.003	-.018
2nd Subjective Component (V9)	.250		
3rd Subjective Component (V10)	-.023		
1981 Services Employment	.287		-.903**
1981 Manufacturing Employment (%) (V12)	1.110*	-.780**	
1961-71 Population Change (V13)	.296	-.037	-.102
1981 Functional Index (V14)		-.412	
1981 Participation Rate (V15)		-.056	
1971-81 TS 'Old' (V16)		.060	
1971-81 Change in Functional Index (V17)		-.631*	-.194**
1971-81 Change in Primary Employment (V18)		-.022	
1971-81 TS 'Medium' (V19)			.085
1971-81 Change in Manufacturing Employment (V20)			.023
1971-81 Population Change (V21)			
R^2	.430	.756	.774
X^2	16.748	18.905	15.405

Note, ß significant: * $t_{.05}$; ** $t_{.01}$

remaining significant ßs both have inverse connotations, which is to say, population gain is taking place outside of the region's transportation centres (perhaps an insight into the declining role of railway branch lines) and it is not present in those communities cursed with high levels of unemployment. The other regressors - standard indicators of infrastructure and well-being - failed to emerge as significant in the model, as did the metropolitan proximity factor. It would appear, therefore, that the communities in our sample within striking distance of Winnipeg are not benefiting from any undue population spill-over effects. This finding is at odds with what might have been expected *a priori*, not to mention the plot of population change and distance (Figure 3.2) which suggests a tendency for demographic stagnation with increasing isolation from the region's metropolis.

For its part, Equation 2 identifies the principal factors coming to bear on the service sector. Of overwhelming import is the linkage with manufacturing and, what is more, its inverse character. In other words, communities enjoying substantial manufacturing employment are not the traditional central places. The implication is that the presumed stimulating effect of industry upon services (à la economic-base theory) is not effective in Manitoba, at least inasmuch as measurable employment impacts are concerned. The only other significant ß is that applying to the 'change in functional index' variable. By virtue of its inverse standing, it suggests that the upgraded commercial status of a community is not conducive to enhanced service employment. Two important implications follow from such an assertion: first, that expansion in the commercial service sector is being undertaken as a capital-intensive rather than a labour-intensive process indeed, commercial upgrading appears to adversely affect job creation and, secondly, that the increasing service-orientation of a community must fall, by default, to the job-creating activities of the public sector (i.e., social services).

The reciprocity between services and manufacturing is also the hallmark of Equation 3. Now, manufacturing employment is inversely related to services in the mirror image of Equation 2. Supplementing this relationship, however, are two other meaningful ones. In the first place, the V17 result suggests that boosted commercial status is not inducing job creation - via the demand intermediary - in the manufacturing sector. In other words, it endorses the fundamental gulf between the two economic sectors in their distribution among the set of small towns.

Table 3.6 Subjective Component Constituents

Variable	Loadings V8	V9	V10
S_1 % respondents preferring small towns for grocery shopping	.260	.281	-.704
S_2 % respondents preferring small towns for liquor, lumber and banking needs	.196	.441	-.064
S_3 % respondents preferring small towns for furniture, appliances, clothing and cars	.266	.435	-.107
S_4 % respondents preferring small towns for veterinary, dental and legal requirements	.121	.450	.318
S_5 % respondents preferring small towns for health-care facilities	.281	.299	.560
S_6 Index of degree of satisfaction	.398	-.222	-.058
S_7 Index of feelings of future potential	.397	-.140	-.135
S_8 Index of involvement in community affairs	.384	-.270	.060
S_9 Index of participation in commmunity organizations	.341	-.222	.220
S_{10} Index of leadership quality	.386	-.234	.018
Variance	50.92	27.32	7.54

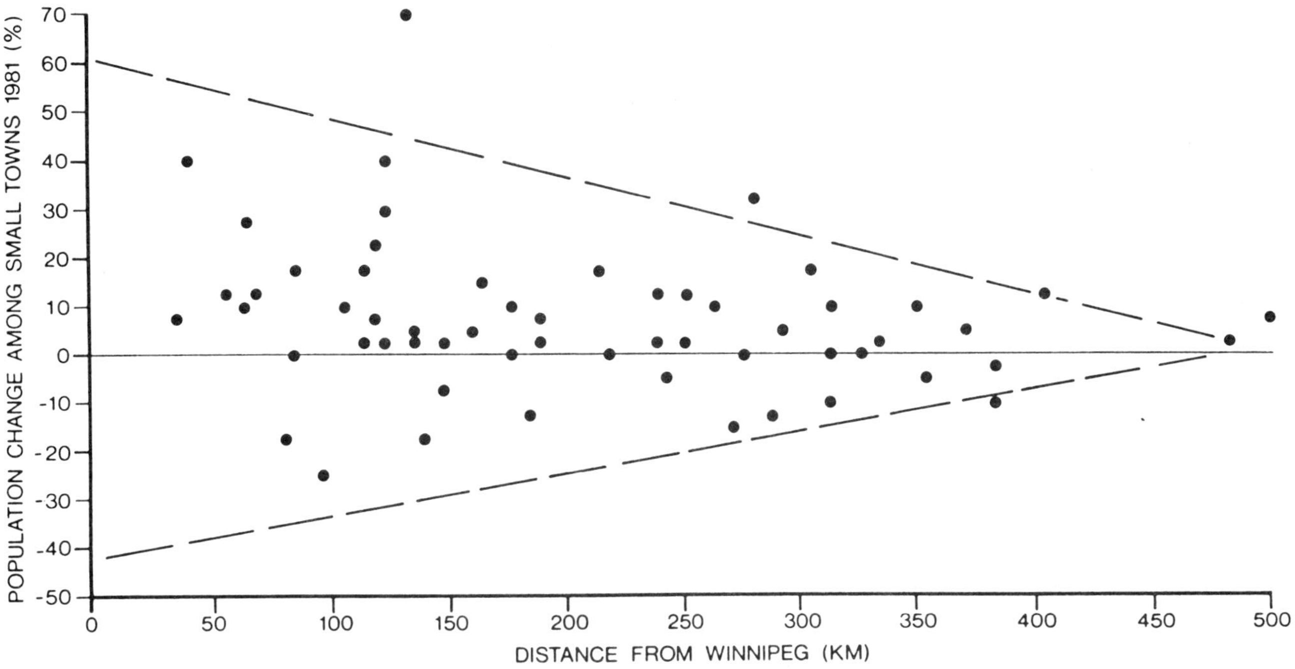

Figure 3.2 Population Change Relative to Metropolitan Proximity.

Secondly, the inverse relationship with distance to Winnipeg conforms to the well-known distance-decay effect. Put simply, transplanted factories (and, indeed, local 'seedbed' manufacturing) are found in the communities close to Winnipeg but with increasing scarcity elsewhere.

The R^2 goodness-of-fit indicators and the Chi-square test of residuals (homoscedasticity) are promising enough to justify accepting the model specifications as depicted. However, the failure of certain expected relationships to emerge therein as significant determinants is surprising. In particular, the continued relevance of the agricultural base is called into question. The insignificant relationship between the change in primary employment and the level of service activity displayed in Equation 2 suggests that rural-farm populations are no longer a crucial factor in setting the threshold levels for small-town service activities. Equally, the first-order correlation between manufacturing employment and the change in primary employment (-.007) hints at the irrelevance of declining rural-farm populations to the presence of manufacturing in small towns. It would appear, therefore, that small-town economic activities are becoming more autarkic relative to the surrounding farm economy. The consequences of this trend will be explored in the following chapters, especially in terms of providing for the social needs of small-town populations (Chapter 4) and formulating policies for steering the direction of changes through which such communities must pass (Chapter 5).

Chapter 4

Social Factors and Truncation

Community satisfaction is essentially a social phenomenon which determines the degree to which small towns are tolerable places in which to live. As the model brought out in Chapter 3, such social concerns are meaningful in understanding the factors at work in promoting population change among the small towns of Agro-Manitoba. Indeed, the crucial connection between quality-of-life (a generally social factor) and the level of service provision (an economic factor) is well established (Stevens, 1980). The presence of services affords economic stability and even expansion on the one hand (Smith, 1985), while fulfilling the vital social function of meeting the needs of rural residents on the other. This latter concern is especially telling for Agro-Manitoba where there exist many communities endowed with disproportionate numbers of old people. The object of this chapter is to focus on such communities, the so-called truncated settlements, and discuss the availability of services within them.

Several findings from the previous chapter are germane to the social themes that are to be subsequently developed. First, and foremost, is the proposition that towns are becoming increasingly independent of the farm economy. A natural rider of this changing state of affairs is the requirement that the service offerings of towns must be geared less to fulfilling the traditional agricultural 'back-up' role and more to providing townspeople with a range of facilities attuned to their specific needs. In this respect, a second finding comes to the fore, namely, the discrepancy between service provision and manufacturing development in the region's communities. Thus, those communities benefiting from manufacturing expansion are not gaining a commensurate endowment of services relative to what is available in other non-manufacturing centres. In part, this situation is a lag effect, since manufacturing growth is of recent occurrence and the upgrading of services has scarcely had time to come to fruition. However, it also reflects the fact that many services in the small-town sector are geared to the peculiar needs of truncated communities and are borne as necessary public services by the province at large. In a real sense, then, they are liberated from the requirement of meeting a 'commercial' threshold.

The invigoration of manufacturing among a sprinkling of the small towns highlights the paradoxical effects of metropolitan proximity. On the one hand, population growth throughout the small-town sector is barely influenced by distance to Winnipeg, although the gravitation of manufacturing to those communities near to the provincial capital is. The difference, evidently, arises out of the relative paucity of manufacturing growth in the region's small-town system. Unlike the rest of Canada where metropolitan spread effects are of sufficient stature to generate significant growth around the major metropolitan centres (Hodge and Qadeer, 1983; Stone, 1980), the same cannot be said for Manitoba. It is apparent, therefore, that those communities at some remove from Winnipeg and bereft of manufacturing must rely on services for their future viability in lieu of the stimulus afforded by manufacturing. What is more, the structural constraint imposed on commercial services following from the need to attain profitable thresholds, puts the onus in these towns on their ability to provide public services geared to social equity ends.

Distance was also presumed to have some bearing on the results of the shift-share analysis. It was gleaned from the SSA that truncated communities were characterized by negative residual shifts. This was construed as representing the 'isolation' factor and, in light of the aforementioned discussion on manufacturing distribution, is sustainable as such. The equally telling fact that truncated communities are so identified as a result of their unbalanced age cohorts, also reinforces the view that the lack of 'active' age groups is attributable to a scarcity of manufacturing jobs. It is reasonable, therefore, to claim that the absence of economic diversification (manufacturing for the most part) ultimately conspires to produce truncated communities, of which this region has a large number.

Truncation, then, is the state to which most rural small towns will gravitate if manufacturing development is checked or curtailed. It can be staved off over the short- to medium-term by a reinvigorated service sector, but failure to address this issue can only result in what Jane Jacobs has called the lot of 'deserted' rural settlements, namely, "the old looking after the old" (Jacobs, 1984). Indeed, the 'aging' of rural towns and villages is often tacitly taken as being inevitable. Not only are the elderly left behind when the young seek their fortunes elsewhere, but also the attachment to an area that comes with longstanding familiarity - what Goldscheider (1971) terms the integration approach - tends to actively inhibit elderly relocation away from rural areas (Fernandez and Dillman, 1979). Furthermore, some elderly are relocating to small towns in preference to retirement in their native cities. They are doing so in response to the notion that those services which give a better quality-of-life occur in smaller communities (Biggar, 1980; Fuguitt and Tordella, 1980; Gober and Zonn, 1983; Wiseman, 1980; Wiseman and Roseman, 1979). Certainly, U.S. evidence points to the intrinsic attractiveness of services for those rural communities that are experiencing population 'turnaround.' Such mundane considerations as police protection, paved roads, adequate water, sewage, health care and schools, all contribute to the forces inducing people to relocate into rural settlements (Goodwin et al, 1984).

Truncation versus Non-Truncation

It is worth recollecting that while the majority of settlements in the representative sample of 58 Agro-Manitoba towns made population gains between 1971 and 1981, most of that growth was ascribable to the intermediate- and old-age categories. The minuscule total of five settlements recording positive total shifts for the young category highlights the dichotomy between population growth *per se* and *balanced* population growth. Those five settlements in question are the truly non-truncated communities. Theirs is the condition of population 'turnaround' combined with generally vibrant growth of both manufacturing and service employment, not to speak of locations that are within striking distance of the metropolitan centre (Table 4.1). By way of contrast, the most acute recorders of +TS for the older cohort have as much chance of losing overall population as gaining it, show no marked propensity either way to gain or lose manufacturing and service employment, but are located, in the main, at greater distances from the metropolitan centre.

Table 4.1 Agro-Manitoba: Summary Characteristics of Truncated and Non-Truncated Communities

Type	Mean distance to Winnipeg	Propensity - as determined by residuals from equations 1-3 (a) Population Growth	(b) Service Growth	(c) Manufacturing Growth
Non-truncated	137	5/5	3/5	4/5
Acute truncated	183	7/10	5/10	6/10
Intermediate[1]	156	15/23	14/23	15/23
Mean distance for all communities to Winnipeg	208	-	-	-

Note: 1. Defined as those communities scoring +TS on the intermediate cohort. Note further, it includes all five of the 'non-truncated' settlements.

Table 4.2 Agro-Manitoba: Elderly Dependency Ratios for Small Towns, 1981

Settlement Size	EDR for growing communities (average, %)	EDR for declining communities (average, %)
<1000	30.7	32.2
1000-1999	27.4	27.1
2000-2999	28.5	29.7
3000-3999	25.5	33.4
4000-4999	25.5	-
5000-9999	18.7	27.1
10,000-35,000	18.3	-
Winnipeg	14.7	-
Manitoba	15.5	-

A convenient handle for grasping the truncation phenomenon is the elderly dependency ratio (EDR). Computed simply as the ratio of people aged 65 and over in comparison to those aged between 15 and 64, the EDR provides a succinct indication of the balance among adult townspeople between those formally out of the actual or potential workforce and those still within it. Obviously, the larger the EDR the greater the burden imposed on the gainfully employed and the more specialized the community's services will need to be tailored to the needs of the elderly. Not surprisingly in view of the SSA findings, the EDR is alarmingly higher for all of Agro-Manitoba's rural small towns and villages (not just the sample of 58) than it is for Winnipeg or for the province as a whole (Table 4.2). What is apparent, however, is the tendency of EDRs to decline with increase in size of small towns. In particular, communities of less than 1000 are most prone to truncation as their EDRs are on average twice that experienced by the provincial metropolis. Equally telling, whereas EDRs are generally higher for declining settlements than they are for growing ones, the disparity between the two groups is inconsequential when put alongside the glaring gap between metropolitan and non-metropolitan EDRs. The distinction is not simply one of scale - higher-order versus lower-order functions beloved of central-place theory - but is primarily that of kind, whereby small-town services are much more oriented towards public goods than are the services found in cities. The inability of many truncated communities to meet commercial thresholds for services becomes almost immaterial owing to the pressing need to provide for the health-care, convenience, and other social requirements of their disadvantaged, dependent populations.

To all intents and purposes, Manitoba's truncated settlements conform to type, namely, the "communities left behind" which are scattered across the Great Plains, both in the U.S. and Canada (Rogerson, 1984; Whiting, 1974). Of the eleven incorporated settlements found within the 50 km commuting belt around Winnipeg, no fewer than ten experienced absolute population growth in recent years. At 23.9%, the average EDR for the eleven Manitoba settlements in question is considerably lower than the 30.4% pertaining to those settlements falling outside of the belt. Consequently, it is reasonable to suppose that retirement relocation to Agro-Manitoba's small towns located around Winnipeg is of less significance than the growth derived from the settlement of labour-force active people who commute to the city.

Services and Population Needs

While a partial correlation coefficient of .61 (significant at the .01 level) between the 1981 population of Agro-Manitoban settlements and the functional indices of the settlements confirms the continuing dependence of townspeople and commercial businesses on each other, the recent disruption in the secular decline of rural communities has played havoc with the regularity of this relationship. Functional indices for declining communities are likely to be higher than those for recently expanding ones (Table 4.3). This supports the proposition that growing communities may be exploiting a new economic base (in a word, manufacturing) which seemingly has little interdependence with services or alternatively, requires a greater transitional period to allow for reassertion of the balance between the new base and services. This empirical regularity bears up even when non-commercial services are brought into the equation. Construction of a social infrastructure index (see Chapter 2 and Appendix 2.1) as a composite measure of the existence of health, recreation, cultural, housing and educational facilities, is noteworthy in its propensity to display a better endowment for declining communities than in growing communities (Table 4.3). Not only does this reaffirm the separation of manufacturing and services within the small-town sector, but it suggests that declining communities - truncated, to all intents and purposes - have a wealth of social overhead capital disproportionate to their current population standing. That endowment of social infrastructure is the combined result of a residue of facilities inherited from the 'non-truncated' past and a recent accretion of facilities geared to the particular needs of the elderly dependent population.

Table 4.4 indicates the contrasting scales for three types of rural setting. It elicits, first of all, that community satisfaction is higher in the more urbanized environments. Indeed the economic indicator mirrors the gradation of rurality, with rural-farm elderly perceiving themselves to be worse off than those in small communities of less than 1000 population, who in turn do not regard themselves as highly placed on this factor as do townspeople. Secondly, differences between the three environments are significant and this is especially so between rural-farm

Table 4.3 Agro-Manitoba: Variations in Service Indicators, 1981

Settlement	Average Functional Index for communities:		Average Social Infrasturucture Index for communities:	
	Growing	Declining	Growing	Declining
<1000	.204	.181	.279	.299
1000-1999	.349	.432	.397	.424
2000-2999	.553	.699	.491	.520
3000-3999	.747	.733	.649	.511
4000-4999	.550	-	.463	-
5000-9999	.907	1.230	.642	.746
10,000-35,000	2.554	-	.783	-

Table 4.4 Agro-Manitoba: Community Satisfaction Among the Elderly

Indicators of community satisfaction	Rural-Farm oriented community (mean value)	Village (<1000 population) community (mean value)	Rural-Town dominated community (mean value)
Psycho-social 1.29	1.18	1.16	
Shelter	1.48	1.32	1.32
Household maintenance, food and clothing	1.24	1.09	1.08
Ethno-cultural	1.44	1.39	1.39
Physical health functioning	1.50	1.27	1.24
Mental health functioning	1.57	1.30	1.25
Proximity of family, friends and familiar community	1.62	1.75	1.68
Availability of family, friends and familiar community as resources	1.07	.98	.98
Economic	1.42	1.30	1.20
t test		1.18[1]	.35[1]

Note: 1. Significant at .01 and .05 level.

Source: Derived from information in, *Aging in Manitoba: Needs and Resources*, 1971, Vol. 3.

elderly and the older residents of the smaller towns. Evidently, a clear distinction exists in the level of community satisfaction expressed by farm dwellers and the inhabitants of urban settlements, regardless of size. Conversely, differences between villages and towns are less pronounced than those between farm dwellers and villagers. Reversing this trend is the economic factor where respondents register higher satisfaction in larger communities. Ostensibly, then, it would seem that the more rural older people appreciate the closer social ties of smaller rural communities while expressing dissatisfaction with the range of available economic benefits, whereas the older townspeople appreciate the better economic opportunities of the larger communities even though that carries with it an erosion of social ties.

A breakdown of the health-services index by size of settlement is salutary (Table 4.4). In the first place, it dichotomizes the communities into those that are categorized as 'truncated' (i.e., with at least double the EDRs prevailing for Winnipeg and the province as a whole) and those which are conveniently classed as 'non-truncated' owing to their EDRs conforming to the provincial average. Secondly, the average indicators for the commercial functional index and health-services index are contrasted for each size class between the truncated (T) and non-truncated (NT) settlements. Two observations are apparent: first, that the magnitude of both indices rises with increasing settlement size irrespective of the T:NT dichotomy and, secondly, that NT-settlements have inferior index values with the notable exception of the towns in the 3000-3999 size class.These differences appear to vindicate what has already been remarked upon herein, namely, that health services in non-truncated communities tend to fall short of the equivalent facilities in truncated communities. Furthermore, the generally superior standing of commercial services in truncated communities below 3000 population is symptomatic of their status as vulnerable units with both shifting economic bases and a susceptibility to population decline (recall Chapter 1). In short, their commercial structure is the residue of a population base which has evaporated by and large to leave a predominantly elderly component which, in the long run, is ill-equipped to underpin those businesses.

The last point makes direct allusion to the tendency of old people to be relatively poor. Moreover, evidence from the U.S. emphatically indicates that the

Table 4.5 Agro-Manitoba: Public Housing Allocation

Urban size class	Public Housing Index Average for:	
	T	NT communities
< 1000	.286	.184
1000-1999	.286	.437
2000-2999	.375	.549
3000-3999	.515	.485

incidence of poverty among the old is particularly evident in small communities (Johansen and Fuguitt, 1984). Not only are the elderly removed for the most part from the workforce, but they are frequently denied the support from their offspring because of out-migration of the younger cohorts (although it is recognized that absent family members often support their parents through remittances). Correspondingly, the rural elderly in the U.S. rely more on social security than their city counterparts, they report lower overall incomes, poorer health and more restricted mobility (Youmans, 1980). Lack of public transport is a prominent irritant, especially among older women who find their access to small-town services hindered as a result of either its absence or its prevalence only at inconvenient, 'rush-hour' times (Auerbach, 1976; Patton, 1975). Indeed, the effectiveness of social services in towns may be considerably undermined simply because of the immobility of many of the elderly and this, in turn, courts the danger of reducing their utilization rates (Windley, 1983).

Poverty rebounds directly on housing. Table 4.5 supports the view that communities most in need of subsidized housing, truncated settlements, have generally fared worse than non-truncated communities in the allocation of public housing. In fact, only the truncated communities of less than 1000 residents and towns in excess of 3000 people have received endowments of public housing better than those destined for non-truncated communities. As the former are most susceptible to population decline, the provision of public subsidies in the housing area is at least symbolic of the Government's intention to reverse the erosion of their populations. Clearly, the Government is attempting to balance the distribution of scarce resources: on the one hand it must attempt to meet the needs of elderly people, but, on the other, it must provide for the needs of young families.

Conclusion

Services are a vital constituent of the fabric of Agro-Manitoba's small towns. They serve not merely as adjuncts to the economic system, complementing agriculture (decreasingly) and manufacturing (increasingly) in their role as non-basic spin-offs of the rural economy, but also as crucial supports of the rural social system. Without an adequate provision of services, life would become intolerable. This function of providing a 'life-support system' is accentuated in the case of dependent populations, primarily the elderly. As a region characterized by a preponderance of truncated communities, Agro-Manitoba has a challenge in attempting to fulfill the special needs of its elderly population. Consequently, today, services are not so much business enterprises as they are social/public goods. Indeed, they should be conceived as verging on the pure public goods category, that is, they may have to be provided to rural communities on the grounds of social equity regardless of the ability of those communities to meet either their capital or operating costs.

Chapter 5

A Perspective on Prairie Small Towns

In accordance with the rest of North America during the 1970s, the study region experienced a pronounced turnaround in its pattern of settlement growth. Small towns collectively increased their population over the 1971-81 intercensal period by 10.9% (Table 5.1) whereas the Winnipeg metropolitan area grew by only 5.5%. In Agro-Manitoba's case it is arguable to what extent the New Democratic government's 'stay option' contributed to this result, as opposed to the prevailing trend of North Americans to be drawn from metropolitan areas by the better quality-of-life that was perceived to exist in rural areas. Nevertheless, our study does indicate that government action, coupled with local initiatives, is important to an appreciation of the fortunes of small towns. On the one hand, many centres have diversified their economic base beyond their initial role of being farm-service communities. The fact that these centres were able to adapt to changing circumstances through the transformation of their functional role by attracting industry and/or modifying their service infrastructure largely accounts for their survival. In this regard, federal and provincial interventions are deemed to play a vital role. On the other hand, some communities with less than 1000 residents failed to alter their economic base sufficiently and tended to stagnate or wither (Table 5.1). However, the future of these smaller centres is unclear, at least at the individual community level, owing to the lack of relationship between rates of population change for the 1961-71 and 1971-81 intercensal periods (Figure 5.1). Table 5.1 reveals another perspective on population change for these two intercensal periods in providing comparisons of centres by functional classification. Of interest is the slowdown in the growth rate of regional centres for the later

Table 5.1 Agro-Manitoba: Population Changes of Small Towns, 1961-1971 and 1971-1981 by Functional Class

Functional Class	Total Population			Percentage Change	
	1961	1971	1981	1961-71	1971-81
1. City (1)*	28,166	31,150	36,242	10.6	16.3
2. Regional Centres (5)	35,240	39,891	42,553	13.2	6.7
3. Market Centres (17)	32,337	35,985	42,086	11.3	17.0
4. Local Centres (34)	25,341	25,576	26,215	0.9	2.5
5. Single-Enterprise Centre (1)	902	667	691	-26.1	3.6
Small Town Total (58)	121,986	133,269	147,787	9.3	10.9

* Number in brackets indicates number of cases.

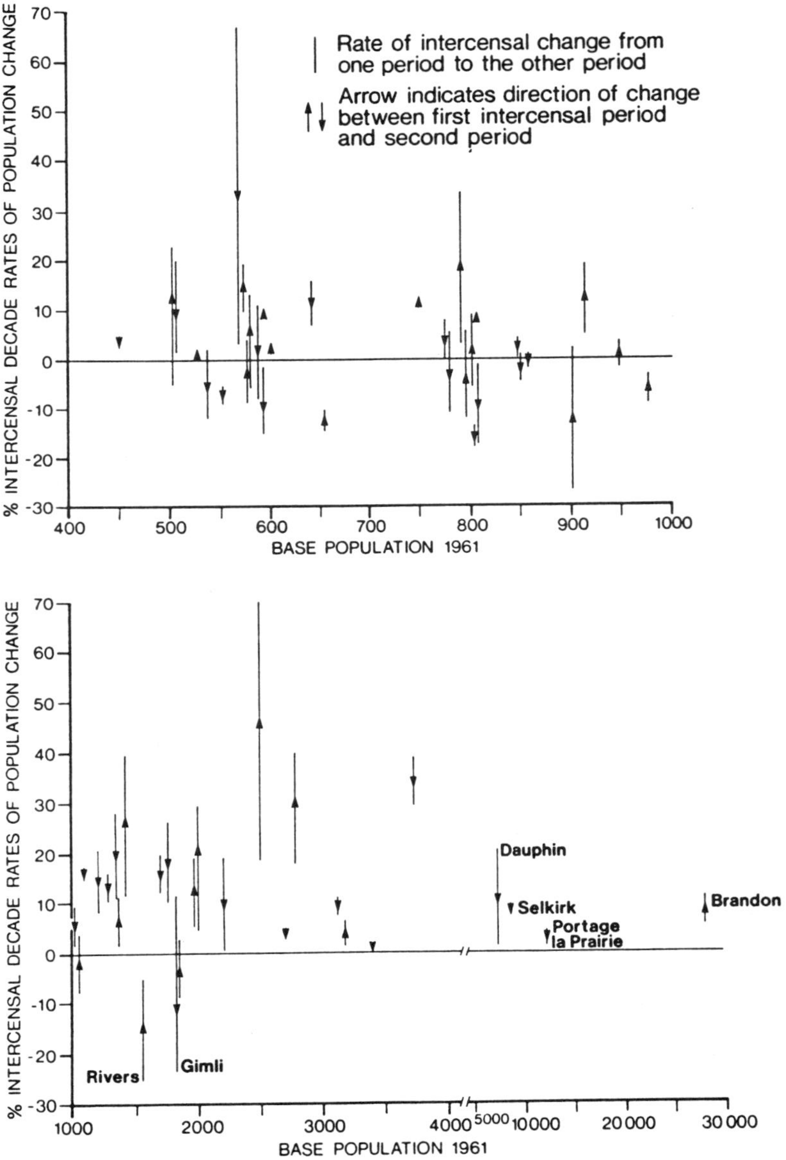

Figure 5.1 Agro-Manitoba: Comparison Between Intercensal Rates of Population Change 1961-1971 and 1971-1981.

period, a phenomenon that appears to have occurred despite the improved rate of growth displayed both by market centres and local centres. These results lend support to the effectiveness of 'stay option' policies.

Where there has been revival of small-town fortunes, it is apparent from our results that the significance of manufacturing cannot be overestimated. In Manitoba, non-metropolitan centre revival and manufacturing resurgence are mutually linked. The precise stimulus to population growth given by manufacturing development is industry specific. In Agro-Manitoba's case, small-town industrialization, which has been aided by regional policies, has been biased towards the sectors of transportation equipment, food processing, agricultural machinery and electrical and electronic equipment (Table 5.2). The table also indicates the grants-per-job disbursed to small towns. Interestingly, it highlights the well-known discrepancy between capital-intensive and labour-intensive industries: i.e. jobs created in the primary metals and chemicals sectors are inordinately more expensive than those following from the expansion of clothing, paper products or transportation equipment. Insofar as job creation in small towns is concerned, the most cost-effective regional policy is one which promotes the latter group of labour-intensive manufacturing. Conversely, capital-intensive jobs are, by their very scarcity and cost, likely to be much more remunerative and, therefore, conducive to widespread income multiplier effects. If rural industrialization is not to degenerate into a process that embellishes cheap-labour businesses, it must temper the garnering of clothing and electronics-assembly plants with a substantial presence of capital-intensive industries. Such a consideration apparently motivated the distribution of regional grants throughout the 1970s.

Manufacturing development and its corollary of job creation depends on investment. Table 5.3 captures the spatial biases in industrial investment displayed within Agro-Manitoba's small towns. The prominence of Brandon reflects its status as the region's major centre outside Winnipeg, whereas Selkirk was singled out as the prime industrial growth centre for the FRED Interlake plan. The presence of Harrowby - a tiny agricultural community - is explained through the location there of a major rapeseed oil-processing plant in the centre of that commodity's harvesting area. Most communities received government support to the extent of a subsidy somewhat less than one-third of total investment. Gimli, however,

Table 5.2 Agro-Manitoba: Manufacturing Jobs Created in Small Towns, 1970-81

Industry	Number of jobs	Cost per job ($)	Regional grant per job ($)
Transportation equipment	1309	9960	4650
Food processing	596	120,250	17,130
Agricultural machinery	396	18,010	5850
Electrical/electronic equipment	389	25,910	6910
Wood products	302	18,740	6070
Clothing	299	4960	1770
Miscellaneous products	140	14,500	4620
Plastics	48	12,000	5170
Paper products	41	9850	2950
Fabricated metal products	30	122,000	25,570
Non-metallic mineral products	26	91,770	19,310
Chemicals	26	1,168,270	120,270
Primary metals	25	1,304,120	149,520
Textiles	21	90,430	19,900
Printing	14	82,290	14,290
Furniture	10	27,300	8300
Misc. petroleum/coal products	5	55,000	15,000

Source: Derived from Dept. of Regional Economic Expansion releases, 1970-1981.

Table 5.3 Agro-Manitoba: Industrial Investment in Small Towns, 1970-81

Community[1]	Investment $ ('000)	Proportion of investment owing to regional grants (%)
Brandon	37,327	13
Selkirk	36,585	13
Harrowby	29,800	9
Portage la Prairie	21,070	22
Winkler	8815	34
Altona	7051	14
Rockwood (vicinity of Winnipeg)	4522	27
Steinbach	3174	24
Gimli	2935	92
Morden	2092	33
Teulon	2092	23
Carman	2074	22
Rivers	2066	30
Morris	2048	46
Dauphin	1837	32
Blumenort	1747	16

Note: 1. Only those acquiring in excess of $1 million are recorded.

warranted a much higher subsidy by virtue of its role as the core growth centre for the Interlake and the recipient of an aerospace plant which failed in December 1975 despite its having received considerable provincial monies. The collapse of this brave attempt to graft high-tech industry into a rural community accounts for the paradoxical showing of Gimli in the model, whereby the residuals from Equation 1 intimate that its population change between 1971 and 1981 was worse than expected (Table 5.1). Overall, however, communities performing better than predicted by the model were also beneficiaries of significant manufacturing investment indeed, some (Carman, Winkler and Teulon) figure prominently in the list drawn up in Table 5.3. Conversely, communities performing worse than expected in terms of population growth did so either in spite of sizeable manufacturing employment within them (Powerview, Carberry and the aforementioned Gimli) or, as a result of a disproportionate number of elderly people with high mortality rates (the rest).

Aided by government largesse, manufacturing will likely consolidate its position in Manitoba's small towns. The continued need to tap cheaper labour supplies combined with the erosion of agglomeration advantages for manufacturing (Garnick, 1984), leads us to suggest that the potential for economic diversification of these communities has scarcely been met. The major disabilities of limited market accessibility and a stunted manufacturing tradition can be offset by cheap energy, relatively cheap labour and the continued reduction in real terms of transport costs. Government has little choice but to continue to support manufacturing development in the more promising small towns in order to redress the problems of truncation. With the EDRs double the rate of the cities the majority of small towns are in danger of terminal decay. While the province has undertaken a measured programme of public-service provision geared specially to the needs of the elderly the failure of such services to generate either a substantial number of permanent new jobs or stimulate local manufacturing initiatives serves to underline the social equity basis of its intervention. Notwithstanding the acclamations of the 'stay option' and TED, serious attempts at coordinating permanent job-creation projects (e.g. grants to manufacturing firms) with those of a 'public-goods' flavour have not been forthcoming. Clearly, there is a need to select communities which can satisfactorily undertake both functions. These centres would aspire to become 'development centres' capable of jointly fulfilling several objectives, by accommodating the rural elderly and providing them with a whole range of health-care and recreation services, providing jobs for those younger people willing to relocate to the city and, in the long run, might inspire local enterprise to create local business rather than rely on outside capital for manufacturing initiatives with the inherent uncertainty which is thereby implied. But the majority of the small towns will continue to house a disproportionately large elderly population until the natural course of events reduces the imbalance and, in so doing, serves to shrink their aggregate population. The impossibility of having manufacturing investment directed to all such communities, as well as the inability of the shrinking farm population to bolster their commercial base, offers most rural settlements little prospect other than that of gentle, secular decline.

This study may have important implications for other areas where agriculture remains the dominant economic activity. Both in Canada and the United States the general consensus is that farm size will continue to increase over the next two decades, albeit (according to some experts) at a slower rate than in previous decades owing to reductions in the rate of change in capital-using technology (Veeman and Veeman, 1984; Jones and Tung, 1984). Particular concern is expressed for the prospects of farmers in the U.S. Great Plains who have benefited from price supports and subsidies that in 1985 were reduced by the U.S. Secretary for Agriculture. After several recent years of economic hardship for farmers, this action will only accelerate "American agriculture toward a destiny of fewer and larger farms" as farmers are confronted by increased debt, and rising costs but falling prices (Robbins, 1985). As indicated throughout this study, the loss of farms serves to disengage the fortunes of small towns from agriculture, so that survival hinges largely upon their ability to diversify. Owing to the limited number of resource options open to these communities, the recommended option is in attracting manufacturing branch plants to locate in them. In view of the intense inter-community competition for such branch plants, it is important that governments intervene to support such establishment in selected towns as part of an overall plan of regional development aimed at reducing, if not eliminating, rural disparities. Where truncated communities have evolved, then it must be recognized that not all can survive indefinitely, in particular those with the characteristics of a local centre are likely to decline unless situated in close proximity to a metropolitan area, city or regional centre. Here again government can be instrumental in providing selected centres with the social services and amenities appropriate for the elderly as an integral part of comprehensive regional planning.

Finally, our clarion call is that government not retrench their involvement in regional planning, as currently seems to be the vogue, but actively embrace the challenges posed by rural development and small-town futures with long-term policies that recognize both the importance of manufacturing and the needs of the elderly.

APPENDIX 2.1

I. Basic Infrastructure

i) Utility services

Index determined by consideration of either the presence of or level of the following services: electricity, natural gas, telephone, bulk oil dealership, sewage system and water supply.

ii) Transportation services

Index based on the following criteria: condition and access of community by roads; frequency or absence of railroad service; aerodrome quality and level of air-scheduled services; and level of bus and truck traffic.

iii) Protection and administrative services

Index based on following criteria: judicial services including level of police protection and presence of criminal or civil courts; fire-fighting service; ambulance service; and level of provincial administrative services (number of offices associated with specific branches of governments).

II. Social Infrastructure

i) Educational facilities

Index calculated on a range of educational facilities present in a community from kindergarten to post-secondary institutions.

ii) Health facilities

Index determined by the size and number of extended-care hospital facilities, acute general hospitals and medical nursing units, along with the number of physicians.

iii) Cultural facilities

Index based on the occurrence and number of libraries, museums, theatres and halls.

iv) Recreational facilities

Index determined by the occurrence and number of arenas/ice rinks, swimming pools, gymnasia, playing fields, curling rinks and additional facilities, such as tennis courts and bowling alleys.

v) Public and aged/infirm housing

Index used a rating system of the number of public housing per 100 population and for the aged/infirm housing and personal care units per 100 population.

Service Infrastructure

The service index (SI) is combined measure of diversity and choice of services provided in a community. It was determined by the formula

$$SI = \frac{D \cdot C}{Dmax} \times \frac{1}{100}$$

Where D = diversity of services
C = choice, or total number of services
Dmax = maximum number of services (30)

Source: Extracted from Manitoba, Department of Industry and Commerce, *Regional Analysis Program Southern Manitoba* Working Paper No.3, Analysis of Community Services and Facilities, Winnipeg, 1974.

APPENDIX 3.1 Variables Used in Small-Town Economic Model

Variable	Composition
V1: Health Index 1981	Computed in comparable manner to 1971 (see Appendix 2.1)
V2: Education Index 1981	" " " "
V3: Transport Infrastructure 1981	" " " "
V4: Average Income 1980	Average personal taxable income
V5: % Unemployment 1981	Average for the year
V6: TS 'Young'	Derived from SSA (see Ch. 3)
V7: Metropolitan proximity	Road distance in km.
V8: lst Subjective Component	Scores from principal components analysis (Ch. 3)
V9: 2nd Subjective Component	" " " "
V10: 3rd Subjective Component	" " " "
V11: % Services Employment 1981	(Service employment/Total Employment) ·100
V12: % Manufacturing Employment 1981	(Manufacturing employment/Total Employment)·100
V13: Population Change 1961-71	((1971 pop - 1961 pop)/1961 pop)·100
V14: Functional Index 1981	Standard central place index utilising commercial outlets only
V15: Participation Rate 1981	Average (%) for year
V16: TS 'Old'	Derived from SSA (see Ch. 3)
V17: Change in Functional Index	1981 FI - 1971 FI
V18: Change in Primary Employment	((1981 PE - 1971 PE)/1971 PE) ·100
V19: TS 'Intermediate'	Derived from SSA (see Ch. 3)
V20: Change in Manufacturing Employment	((1981 ME - 1971 ME)/1971 ME) ·100
V21: Population Change 1971-81	((1981 pop - 1971 pop)/1971 pop) ·100

REFERENCES

Artibise, A. F. J. 1979. "The Urban West: The Evolution of Prairie Towns." *Prairie Forum,* 4, (2), pp. 237-262.

Averitt, R. T. 1979. "Implications of the Dual Economy for Community Economic Change," in *Nonmetropolitan Industrial Growth and Community Change.* Summers, G.F. and Selvik, A. (D.C. Heath, Lexington), pp. 71-91.

Biggar, J. C. 1980. "Who Moved Among the Elderly, 1965 to 1970: a Comparison of Types of Older Moves" *Research on Aging,* 2, pp. 73-91.

Brierley, J. S. and Todd, D. 1978. "Agricultural and Urban Interaction in Southern Manitoba: a Canonical Analysis." *Canadian Journal of Agricultural Economics,* 26, (2), pp. 43-54.

Brunner, E. and Lorge, I. 1937. *Rural Trends in the Depression Years* (McGraw-Hill, New York).

Canada. 1956. *Royal Commission on Canada's Economic Prospects* (Queen's Printer, Ottawa).

Canada/Manitoba. N.d. *A Decade of Development in the Interlake* (Department of Regional Economic Expansion and Department of Agriculture, Winnipeg).

Canada, Ministry of State for Economic and Regional Development. 1984. *Manitoba Economic Development Perspective 1984* (Winnipeg).

Dahms, F. A. 1980. "The evolving Spatial Organization of Small Settlements in the Countryside - An Ontario Example." *Tijd. voor Econ. en Soc. Geografie,* 71, pp. 295-306.

Dale, E. H. 1977. "The General Problems of Western Canada's Small Rural Towns;" *Regina Geographical Studies.* University of Regina, Department of Geography, pp 87-100.

Dawson, C. A and Younge, E. R. 1940. *Pioneering in the Prairie Provinces: The Social Side of the Settlement Process* III, Canadian Frontiers of Settlement, eds. Mackintosh, W. A. and Joerg, W. L. G. (MacMillan, Toronto).

Economic Council of Canada. 1984. *Western Transition* (Minister of Supply and Services, Ottawa).

Erickson, R. A. 1976. "The Filtering-down Process: Industrial Location in a Nonmetropolitan Area." *The Professional Geographer*, 28, pp. 254-260.

Fernandez, R. R. and Dillman, D.A. 1979. "The Influence of Community Attachment on Geographic Mobility." *Rural Sociology*, 44, pp. 345-360.

Fuguitt, G. V. 1972. "Some Demographic Aspects of the Small Town in the United States." *Sociologis Ruralis*, 12, (2), pp.147-159.

Fuguitt, G. V. and Tordella, S. J. 1983. "Elderly Net Migration." *Research on Aging*, 2, pp. 38-43.

Garnick, D. H. 1984. "Shifting Balances in U.S. Metropolitan and Nonmetropolitan Area Growth." *International Regional Science Review*, 9, pp. 257-273.

Giles, J. D. 1978. *ARDA in Manitoba* (Manitoba, Department of Agriculture, Winnipeg).

Gober, P. and Zonn, L. E. 1983. "Kin and Elderly Amenity Migration." *The Gerontologist*, 23, pp. 288-294.

Goldscheider, C. 1971. *Populationn, Modernization and Social Structure* (Little, Brown and Co., Boston).

Goodwin, H. L. et al. 1984. "Determination of Settlement Patterns in Rapidly Growing Rural Areas." *Annals of Regional Science*, 18, pp. 67-80.

Hansen, N. M. 1974. "Factors Determining the Location of Industrial Activity. In *Rural Lndustrialization: Problems and Potentials*. Ed. Whiting, L. R., (Iowa State University Press, Ames), pp. 27-45.

Hart, J. F. et al. 1968. "The Dying Village and Some Notions about Urban Growth." *Economic Geography*, 44, pp. 343-349.

Hodge, G. 1965. "The Prediction of Trade Centre Viability in the Great Plains." *Papers of the Regional Science Association*, 15, pp. 87-115.

Hodge, G. and Qadeer, M. A. 1983. *Towns and Villages in Canada* (Butterworths, Toronto).

Jacobs, J. 1984. *Cities and the Wealth of Nations: Principles of Economic Life* (Random House, New York).

Johansen, H. E. and Fuguitt, G. V. 1981. "Changing Functions of Villages in Sparsely Populated Areas: The American West." In *Settlement Systems in Sparsely Populated Regions: The United States and Australia*. Eds. Lonsdale, R. E and Holmes, J. H. (Pergamon, New York), pp. 148-168.

Johansen, H. E. and Fuguitt, G. V. 1984. *The Changing Rural Village in America: Demographic and Economic Trends Since 1950* (Billinger, Cambridge, Mass.).

Jones,W. D. and Tung, Fu-Lai 1984. "Farm Numbers and Size ... What's Ahead." *Market Commentary*. In Proceedings of the Canadian Agricultural Outlook Conferences, Dec. 1984 (Agriculture Canada, Ottawa).

Leir, J. 1971. "Farm Mechanization in Saskatchewan. *Tijd, voor Econ. en Soc. Geografie*, 62, (3), pp. 180-189.

Lonsdale, R. E. and Sayler, H. L. eds. 1979. *Nonmetropolitan Industrialization* (Winston, Washington, D.C.).

Mackintosh, W. A., 1934. "Prairie Settlement: The Geographical Setting." I, of *Canadian Frontiers of Settlement*. Eds. Mackintosh, W. A. and Joerg, W. L. G. (MacMillan, Toronto).

Manitoba. 1973 *Guidlines for the Seventies* (Winnipeg).

Manitoba, Commission on Targets for Economic Development. 1969. *Manitoba to 1980* (Winnipeg).

Manitoba, Committee on Manitoba's Economic Future. 1963. *Manitoba 1962-1975* (Winnipeg).

Manitoba, Department of Health and Social Development. 1973. *Aging in Manitoba, Needs and Resources 1971*, 10 volumes (Winnipeg).

Manitoba Department of Industry and Commerce. 1975. *Regional Analysis Program, Southern Manitoba, Part 1A*, Working *Paper No. 1, Socio-demographic Data, Community Interrelations Survey Data* (Winnipeg).

Manitoba, Department of Industry and Commerce. 1975. *Regional Analysis Program Southern Manitoba, Part 2, Working Paper No. 1 Economic Characteristics* (Winnipeg).

Manitoba, Department of Industry and Commerce. 1974. *Regional Analysis Program Southern Manitoba, Part 2, Working Paper No. 2, Analysis of Community Functions and Relationships* (Winnipeg).

Manitoba, Department of Industry and Commerce. 1974. *Regional Analysis Program Southern Manitoba, Part 2, Working Paper No. 3, Analysis of Community Services and Facilities* (Winnipeg).

Manitoba, Department of Industry and Commerce. 1976. *Regional Analysis Program Southern Manitoba, Part 2, Working Paper No. 4, Analysis of Population Change 1951-1971* (Winnipeg).

Patton, C. V. 1975. "Age Groupings Travel in a Rural Area." *Rural Sociology*, 40, pp. 55-63.

Pindyck, R. S. and Rubinfeld, D. L. 1976. *Econometric Models and Economic Forecasts* (McGraw-Hill, New York).

Robbins, W. 1985. "Farm Experts See a Future of Fewer and Larger Tracts." *New York Times*, February 17.

Roepke, H. G. and Freudenberg, D. A. 1981. "The Employment Structures of Nonmetropolitan Counties." *Annals of the American Association of Geographers*, 71, pp. 580-592.

Rogers, D. L. et al. 1978. "Industrialization, Income Benefits, and the Rural Community." *Rural Sociology*, 43, pp. 250-264.

Rogerson, P. A. 1984. "The Demographic Consequences of Metropolitan Population Deconcentration in the U.S." *The Professional Geographer*, 36, pp. 307-314.

Sarbit, L. A. and Greer-Wootten, B. 1980. *Spatial Aspects of Structural Change in Central Place Systems: Southern Manitoba, 1961- 1971* (Geographical Monographs, No. 4, York University).

Sawatzky, H. L. 1970. "Viability of Ethnic Group Settlement, with Reference to Mennonites in Manitoba." *Canadian Ethnic Studies*, 2,(2) pp. 147-160.

Schlichtmann, H. 1977. "Rural Settlements in the Prairie Region of Canada." *Proceedings, Royal Geographical Society of Australia, South Australian Branch*, 78, pp. 29-49.

Smith, S. M. 1985. "Diversifying Small Town Economics with Nonmanufacturing Industries." *Rural Development Perspectives*, 2, (l), pp. 18-22.

Stevens, J. B. 1980. "The Demand for Public Goods as a Factor in the Nonmetropolitan Migration Turnaround." In *New Directions in Urban-Rural Migration: The Population Turnaround in Rural America* Brown, D. L. and Wardwell, J. M. (Academic Press, New York), pp. 115-135.

Stone, L. O. 1980. "Demographic Perspective on Challenges of the 80's." *Transactions of the Royal Society of Canada*, 18, pp. 48-66.

Summers, G. F. 1975. *Industrial Invasion of Nonmetropolitan America: A Quarter Century of Experience* (Praeger, New York).

Todd, D. 1977. "Manufacturing Scale Economics and Community Environments in the Prairie Provinces." (Canada, Department of Regional Economic Expansion, Saskatoon).

Todd, D. 1979. "Regional and Structural Factors in Farm-size Variation: a Manitoba Elucidation." *Environment and Planning A,* 11, pp. 257-269.

Todd, D. and Brierley, J. S. 1977. "Farm Size and Regional Structures: A Preliminary Insight." *Environment and Planning A*, 9, pp. 75-84.

Todd, D. and Brierley, J. S. 1982. "Agricultural Land-use Policies in Prairie Manitoba and the Farm-size Phenomenon." *Geo Journal*, 6, pp. 525-532.

Todd, D. 1983a. "The Small-town Viability Question in a Prairie Context." *Environment and Planning A*, 15, pp. 903-916.

Todd, D. 1983b. "Objective and Subjective Push Factors in Rural Out-migration: A Framework for Analysis." *Rural Systems*, l, pp. 89-106.

Veeman, M. M. and Veeman, T. S. 1984. "Canadian Agriculture in the 1980s." *Current History,* 83, (493), pp. 216-219, 231.

Voisey, P. 1975. "The Urbanization of the Canadian Prairies, 1871-1916." *Histoirie Sociale/Social History,* 8, (15), pp. 77-101.

Wallace, D. B. and Drudy, P. J. 1973. "Social Problems in Rural Communities." In *The Common Agricultural Policy and Britain.* Eds. Rogers, S. T. and Davy, B. H.

Ward, E. N. 1977. *Land-use Programs in Canada-Manitoba* (Environment Canada, Ottawa).

Warren, R.L., 1963, *The Community in America* (Rand McNally, Chicago).

Whiting, L. R., ed. 1974. *Communities left behind: Alternatives for Development*, (Iowa State University Press, Ames).

Windley, P. G. 1983. "Community Services in Small Rural Towns: Patterns of Use by Older Residents." *The Gerontologist*, 23, pp. 180-184.

Wiseman, R. F. and Roseman, C. C. 1979. "A Typology of Elderly Migration Based on the Decision-making Process." *Economic Geography*, 55, pp. 324-337.

Wiseman, R. F. 1980. "Why Older People Move: Theoretical Issues." *Research on Aging*, 2, pp. 141-154.

Zimmerman, C. C. and Moneo, G.V. 1971. *The Prairie Community System* (Agricultural Research Council of Canada, Ottawa).

INDEX

CANADIAN STUDIES

1. Clifford J. Jansen, **Italians in a Multicultural Canada**
2. Dieter Hoehne, **Legal Aid in Canada: From Charity to Public Policy**
3. Satadal Dasgupta, **Rural Canada: Structure and Change**
4. Mark R. Mullins, **Religious Minorities in Canada: A Sociological Study of the Japanese Experience**
5. Joan Vance, **An Analysis of Costs and Benefits of Public Lotteries: The Canadian Experience**
6. Peter A. Russell, **Attitudes To Social Structure and Mobility in Upper Canada 1815-1840**
7. John Brierley, **Prairie Small-Town Survival: The Challenge of Agro-Manitoba**
8. Scott Bennett, **Technology and Work in Canada**